Dr Michelle H. Craig is a Scottish historian at the University of Glasgow, specialising in book and archive history and information studies.

Dr Miles Kerr-Peterson is an independent scholar, primarily interested in early modern Scottish politics, culture and society, but also regional studies related to Scottish Lordship throughout its history.

St Kilda
My Island Home

Christina MacDonald MacQueen

Edited by
MILES KERR-PETERSON AND
MICHELLE H. CRAIG

ORIGIN

First published in 2025 by Origin, an imprint of
Birlinn Limited
West Newington House
10 Newington Road
Edinburgh
EH9 1QS

www.birlinn.co.uk

Editorial material and edition copyright ©
Miles Kerr-Peterson and Michelle H. Craig 2025

Original text copyright © the Estate of
Christina MacDonald MacQueen

All rights reserved. No part of this publication may be
reproduced, stored or transmitted in any form without the express
written permission of the publisher.

ISBN: 978-1-83983-085-3

British Library Cataloguing-in-Publication Data

A catalogue record for this book is available
from the British Library

Typeset by LexisBooks

Papers used by Birlinn Ltd are from well-managed forests and
other responsible sources

Printed and bound by Ashford Colour Limited, Gosport

Contents

Preface	vii
1884–1903: Growing up on St Kilda	1
1903–1929: Leaving St Kilda	6
1929–1930: Evacuation and Christina's Articles	11

St Kilda: My Island Home

PART I	*Hamilton Advertiser*, 7 December 1929	21
PART II	*Hamilton Advertiser*, 14 December 1929	29
PART III	*Hamilton Advertiser*, 21 December 1929	35
PART IV	*Hamilton Advertiser*, 28 December 1929	41
PART V	*Hamilton Advertiser*, 4 January 1930	48
PART VI	*Hamilton Advertiser*, 11 January 1930	54
PART VII	*Hamilton Advertiser*, 18 January 1930	60
PART VIII	*Hamilton Advertiser*, 25 January 1930	66
Interlude	*Hamilton Advertiser*, 1 March 1930	72

My Childhood Days on Lone St Kilda

Article 1	*Dundee People's Journal*, 17 May 1930	79
Article 2	*Dundee People's Journal*, 24 May 1930	84
Article 3	*Dundee People's Journal*, 31 May 1930	90
Interlude	*Hamilton Advertiser*, 31 May 1930	97
Article 4	*Dundee People's Journal*, 7 June 1930	99

Other Articles

Daily Express, 13 June 1930	107
Oban Times, 12 July 1930, Letters to the Editor	110
Interlude Letter from Seamus Chief of Clann Fheargguis of Stra-Chur and Clann Ailpein, 19 July 1930	117
Hamilton Advertiser, 9 August 1930. Robert Chalmers	119
Interlude Letters to the Secretary of State, 7 August and 15 August 1930	125
Oban Times, 23 August 1930. Letters to the Editor	128
Daily Record, 29 August 1930	132
The Scots Magazine: A Monthly Miscellany of Scottish Life and Letters, Volume XV, April 1931–September 1931, 101–103	136
The Scots Magazine: A Monthly Miscellany of Scottish Life and Letters, Volume VI, October 1931–March 1932, 378–383	140

Appendices

Appendix 1	Robert Chalmers' Other *Hamilton Advertiser* Articles	149
Appendix 2	Robert Chalmers, *Sunday Post*, 16 June 1935	157
Appendix 3	Notes on the Images	160
Postscript		163
Bibliography		164
Index		165

Preface

This book was initiated by the late Scott Chalmers (1948–2022), grandson of Christina MacDonald MacQueen. Miles Kerr-Peterson was employed by Scott in his manufacturing businesses, and knowing Miles' background in Scottish history, he brought in a tan-coloured leather trunk, and asked if there was anything important in there.

The trunk was a collection of materials gathered by Janet Chalmers (Christina's daughter, 1916–95, known as 'Jenny'), which passed to her brother David Chalmers (1926–2017) and then his son Robert Chalmers, who had lent them to Scott (a cousin). Nestled within a broad collection of recent St Kilda newspaper clippings was a fragmentary rump of older materials that had belonged to Jenny's mother.

Given the massive literature written about St Kilda over the last century, it is surprising that the writings of Christina MacDonald MacQueen have not been noticed. Much was in the public domain, published in a number of newspapers, although additional and invaluable contextual materials were contained within the trunk. In these we have a former islander writing about herself at the time of the evacuation, and in the context of her own family tragedies that ultimately triggered the abandonment of a millennia-old settlement.

Scott Chalmers, in whose memory this volume is dedicated, died before the completion of the project. He had been suffering from a cocktail of debilitating cancers for almost a decade, but declined sharply over 2022. A sketch biography of Christina, along with a transcription of her writings contained in the trunk did reach him, and his sons were able to read it to him on his deathbed, which apparently bought him some comfort.

Thanks are also expressed to Robert Chalmers, not least as guardian of Jenny's trunk and its valuable contents, but also for lugging said trunk across Scotland on various occasions to make this project possible. Likewise, very hearty thanks are made to Richard ('Bob') Chalmers, Scott's son, for his kind and unwavering support in the finishing of this project.

Thanks are also expressed to John Gillies (great nephew of Christina) and Alasdair MacEachen, who made invaluable comments and corrections on the text, and gave helpful insight identifying individuals in the various photographs. However, any errors remaining in the text belong to the editors.

Only after the original manuscript of this book was submitted was Andrew Fleming's excellent *The Gravity of Feathers* published, which includes an excellent summary of Christina's life. Fleming found some wonderful additional details, not least Reverend James Christie of Carlisle who described Christina in 1905, when she was twenty-one as 'a perfect Venus de Milo'. (*The Gravity of Feathers*, 253–5, 272.)

1884–1903: Growing up on St Kilda

On 10 February 1884 Christina MacDonald MacQueen was born at 10 Main Street, Village Bay, on Hirta.[1] Hirta is the main island of the St Kilda archipelago, and was the only one permanently inhabited. She was born into a small community: three years prior the population of the island was a mere 77 individuals, spread among 19 households.[2] Christina's articles paint the picture of her island home in brighter colours than we can, so we will restrain ourselves in this introduction to outlining her life and childhood up to 1930. We will then continue her story around her writings.

Christina's parents were Marion MacDonald and Donald MacQueen. She was their sixth child, although only the third to survive infancy. From the 1911 census we learn the horrible fact that Marion had given birth to a total of twelve *living* children over her lifetime, with only four surviving to that time (eight died in infancy, two as adults). Infant death plagued St Kilda. There was around a 50 per cent child mortality rate through most of the

---

[1] National Records of Scotland Statutory Register of Births III/4 7. That month the minister of St Kilda, John MacKay, refused to baptise baby Christina, as her father refused to submit to church discipline over some unrecorded infraction. Andrew Fleming, *The Gravity of Feathers: Fame Fortune and the Story of St Kilda* (Birlinn, 2024), 140.
[2] Seventeen of the households were islanders, then there was the Manse with the minister's household, and the Factor's House, which was occupied by Ann MacKinlay, the nurse and teacher.

nineteenth century due to tetanus, compared to industrial Britain's average rate of around 15 per cent.[3] Christina was a very lucky baby. George Murray, the schoolmaster on St Kilda from 1886 to 1887, describes in his diary the agonising illness of baby MacKinnon, a contemporary of Christina: born on 14 December 1886 'Child large and very promising. Mother doing well', but taken ill on the 22nd and died on the 27th. 'In the grave which was opened I saw the coffins of its two little brothers that died the same way.'[4] Christina mentions infant mortality at the end of her article of 28 December 1929, and attributes the cure of the blight to the minister Angus Fiddes, who served on the island from 1889 to 1901, and who took it upon himself to seek midwifery training on the mainland.

Christina was most likely named after Marion's mother, Christina MacKinnon, 1819–87, although Marion also had a sister of the same name who had died in 1880. The name itself was one of the rarer forenames of the island; the more common female names at the time were Catherine, Rachel, Anne and Mary.[5] Marion's father was John MacDonald (1811–89). Christina's paternal grandfather Donald (see below) had died in 1880, while all her other grandparents would be dead by the time she was six years old. However, she would be blessed by having two aunts on her mother's side, Margaret MacDonald (1839–1926) and Catherine MacDonald (1842–1912).

In the 1891 census, we find her in her childhood home as part of a household of six: Donald and Marion with 14-year-old Ann, 11-year-old Norman, 7-year-old Christina and 5-year-old

---

[3] Roger Hutchinson, *St Kilda: A People's History* (Birlinn, 2014), 134.
[4] 'McKinnon' is used here as Murray's spelling, although MacKinnon was the more usual spelling. Murray also records another baby dying of the illness, then in heart-wrenching detail of a girl aged ten. Maureen Kerr, *George Muray: A Schoolteacher for St Kilda, 1886–87* (Islands Books Trust, 2013), 78–82, 90–1, 100.
[5] George Seton, *St Kilda* (Birlinn, 2019), 113. Christina was probably known as 'Kirsty', and this is how Andrew Fleming refers to her in *The Gravity of Feathers*. We have kept the more formal Christina here and Robert rather than 'Bob' for her husband.

Donald. Their little home had only three rooms with windows: two bedrooms and a kitchen. In her article of 14 December 1929, Christina mentions stories by the fireside, and the presence of spinning wheels and a loom hanging from a roof beam. The spinning wheels were used by the women to make thread which Donald wove on the loom. Number 10 Main Street had been built around 1861–68, so was relatively new when Christina was born. It stood immediately adjoining the west side to the little path that led to the circular burial ground, and was almost in the centre of the settlement in Village Bay (see map). In total there were sixteen of these modern houses on Hirta and numerous older dwellings-come-storehouses or byres called 'blackhouses'. At the time of that census three of these blackhouses were still being used as dwellings, such as that of old Rachel MacCrimmon, who Christina describes in her article for the *Scots Magazine*. The whole island spoke Gaelic and her articles show that English was also limited among many of the older generation, such as Rachel.

Christina's father, Donald, was the third in succession to bear that name (while her brother was the fourth and last to be born on Hirta). The first had been born on St Kilda in the mid-eighteenth century. In 1720 and 1727 two epidemics devastated the population of St Kilda, and Christina describes these in detail in her article of 14 December 1929 (although she mistook the year for 1729). Before this great mortality, Hirta's population had been between 180 and 200. After, it was around 42: nine men, ten women, fifteen boys and eight girls. Eleven of the males – three men and eight boys – had been stranded on Stac an Armin over the winter of 1727–28 and escaped the ravages of smallpox. Around twenty-one households had been reduced to four.[6] The feudal superiors of the islands, the MacLeods of Dunvegan, thereafter sent a handful of settlers each year to repopulate the islands. It has been alleged these settlers were felons, sent by the MacLeods as punishment, although this has not been confirmed by contemporary evidence. Christina certainly

---

[6] Hutchinson, *St Kilda*, 83, 86–7.

bristles against the assertion in her letter to the *Oban Times* of July 1930. Among the new settlers was one Finlay MacQueen, although there had been MacQueens on Hirta prior to 1727, and there was even a legend that the first settler on the island was an Irishman called 'Macquin'.[7] Finlay was born sometime around 1695 on Uist. He married a woman with a MacDonald surname, presumably one of the survivors from the pre-epidemic St Kilda families.

Among Finlay's children was a John MacQueen (1750–1830), who married an Ann MacDonald in 1769. One of John's children was Donald MacQueen (1781–1839), who married a Mary MacCrimmon in 1802. Among Donald and Mary's children was the second Donald MacQueen (1804–80), who married a Kirstie Gillies in 1833. An 1860 plan of Village Bay shows a long strip of land in the occupation of Donald MacQueen II, which was to the front of where number 10 would later be built. A 'blackhouse' at its top on Main Street (which survives next to number 10) was his dwelling, built in 1834.[8]

Among Donald II's children was the third Donald MacQueen, born in 1840, Christina's father. In 1862 this Donald had a son with Ann MacDonald. He was the well-known and photographed Finlay MacQueen (1862–1941), master bird catcher and climber. Donald III married Mary Gillies in 1868. She died in 1871. On 2 September 1873, he married Marion MacDonald, Christina's mother.[9] In 1883, the year prior to Christina's birth, Donald was selected, alongside Reverend John MacKay and Angus Gillies, to

---

[7] Mary Harman, *An Isle Called Hirte: a History and Culture of St Kilda to 1930* (MacLean Press, 1997), 130.

[8] Geoffrey Stell and Mary Harman, *Buildings of St Kilda* (RCAHMS, 1988), 4–12.

[9] National Records of Scotland RD:111-03; Hutchinson, *St Kilda*, p.172. Donald III and Mary Gillies had a daughter, Mary Ann MacQueen, born 1871, who married William MacDonald. They had a large family, including Calum MacDonald whose memoir *From Cleits to Castles: A St Kildan Looks Back*, is published by the Islands Book Trust. With thanks to John Gillies for explaining this link.

represent the islanders when the Napier Commission arrived on Hirta to discuss crofting reform. A major grievance was the lack of shipping communication between St Kilda and the rest of Scotland over the winter, something Christina consistently complains about in her articles. Donald was interviewed and spoke confidently on rents, fowling, export prices and the need for a pier to help with fishing.[10]

Christina seems to have had a typical childhood on the island. This is outlined in detail in her articles, although she only briefly mentions her schooling as an aside in her final article. From 1879 a schoolteacher was employed on the island, although few teachers stayed much longer than a year, and their quality varied: one in the late 1890s knew no Gaelic and was hence of little use. From 1890 to 1900 the minister, Angus Fiddes, seems to have borne the responsibility. Schooling took place between the ages of 6 and 14. The schoolhouse was built in 1898, when Christina would have been about 14. Prior to this schooling was probably carried out in the church. The children were taught arithmetic, reading in both Gaelic and English, the history of Scotland, and geography. They were also taught to memorise scripture at Sunday School. From the 1880s the teaching on Hirta had included more English language. Christina would have been one of those described by the visitor Heathcote in 1900 as 'the rising generation who speak it [English] quite well'. This enhanced English education allowed many of the island youth to leave the island for places like Glasgow.[11]

In the 1901 census, taken when Christina was 17 years old, there were eight people living in number 10: Donald III and Marion, and their children, Christina and Donald IV, as well as 9-year-old John and 6-year-old Mary. The couple's eldest son, Norman, who had also been present in 1891, was a 21-year-old, and was also still living at home alongside his 24-year-old wife, also named Christina.

---

[10] Hutchinson, *St Kilda*, 209–11; 219–24.
[11] Hutchinson, *St Kilda*, 207, 217, 234, 242, 268; Harman, *An Isle Called Hirte*, 257; Norman Heathcote, *St Kilda* (Longmans, 1900), 78.

1903–1929: Leaving St Kilda

Christina gives two dates for leaving St Kilda: 1903 in her article for the *Daily Record* (29 August 1930), and 1909 in her article for the *Hamilton Advertiser* (7 December 1929). The circumstances are described in detail in her article for the *Daily Record*. It is not impossible that she left briefly on a trip in 1903, then left again for good in 1909. In her writing Christina explicitly describes a desire to leave the islands and see the world and 'what lay beyond the distant peaks of Harris'. She says, 'I left home because I wanted to. I was the first woman to do so following the clearance of 1855' (although strictly an Ann MacDonald had left in 1889 with minister MacKay, to whom she was servant[12]).

She left a relatively healthy community and a large family. However, both of these circumstances would change in the following decades. On 22 March 1909, her brothers Norman and John drowned when their boat capsized off Dun.[13] This had a noticeably terrible impact on her father, who she says never smiled again. He died soon after, in June 1910. If Christina did leave in

---

[12] Hutchinson, *St Kilda*, 242.
[13] Christina gets the year of this incident wrong in her articles, referring to 1908. The school teacher Alice MacLachlan records it in 1909. David A. Quine, *St Kilda Portraits* (Dowland Press, 1988), 105–6. She refers to John in the Gaelic 'Ian' in her article (although the Gaelic spelling is usually Iain), but keeps Norman anglicised rather than referring to him as 'Tormod'. With thanks to John Gillies for highlighting this.

1909, the deaths of her two brothers, and a desire not to be a burden on her remaining family, may have been a contributing factor: 'the young men and women of the island are just like the young men and women of the glens – they get out as soon as they find themselves a burden on the community.'

Christina was almost certainly helped to settle in Glasgow by Alexander Ferguson (1868–1960), a St Kildan tweed merchant, who lived in the city. Alexander had left Hirta in 1892 and established A.G. Ferguson and Co. St Kilda and Harris Tweed Factors of 93 Hope Street. Alexander's home in Glasgow (in later years in Old Kilpatrick) was usually the first place for St Kildans to stay on leaving the islands and Christina is glowing in her praise for Alexander in her articles.[14] In her piece for the *Daily Express* of 13 June 1930 she describes Alexander's home as 'the St Kildians' employment exchange. Here he has kept them till work was found'.

By the 1911 census, Christina was living as a servant at 2 Bowmont Terrace in Hyndland. This was an ample townhouse in an upmarket part of the city. Her occupation was 'cook, domestic'. She was working for the family of James T Stuart, a machine engineer and tool maker. The home included James' wife Robina, and two daughters: Mary (who at 26 was just a year older than Christina) and Janet (aged 21). Christina was the only member of the household who spoke Gaelic.

A far cry from the crowded bustle of Glasgow, or indeed St Kilda in 1901, number 10 Main Street back on Hirta had just three occupants in the 1911 census: 24-year-old Donald IV, now head of the household, the widowed Marion and 16-year-old Mary. In 1912, the remaining islanders had to appeal for outside help for fear of starvation, which was revealed by a *Daily Mirror* campaign. Soon after the population was laid low by an outbreak of influenza,

---

[14] Hutchinson, *St Kilda,* 268; Donald John Gillies, *The Truth About St Kilda* (Birlinn, 2019) 21.

for which the Royal Navy had to intervene with further supplies and nurses.[15]

On 4 October 1912 Christina married Robert Kinneill Chalmers at Scotstoun Parish Church. Robert Chalmers had been born in Kilbirnie, Ayrshire. His father was David Chalmers (1860–1930) originally from Kinghorn in Fife, a 'Flax Hecklemaker', someone who made tools that prepared flax fibres prior to spinning. His mother was a Janet Mackie (1865–1930) of Inverkeithing. Twenty-four-year-old Robert (four years younger than Christina) was a shipwright living at 19 Somerville Street (now Methill Street) in Scotstoun. It is possible that Robert's father, David Chalmers' connections to the textile industry had put him in contact with Alexander Ferguson's tweed business.

Interestingly, Christina and Robert's marriage seems to have been Church of Scotland. Christina was raised Free Church and the islands had been fiercely attached to this denomination since the 1840s, being one of the main drivers behind the 1852 exodus of 36 St Kildans to Australia.[16]

In 1935, some 23 years after their marriage, Robert wrote an article for the *Sunday Post* (appendix 2) in which he described visiting Hirta in July 1911 with Christina to seek permission for the marriage. It seems that Robert was the first non-St Kildan to visit the island to be vetted in this way. Donald Ferguson had sailed out with them and Robert was suitably inspected and approved by the islanders.[17] Sadly, most of the article is dedicated to describing the terrific storm on the return voyage, instead of delving into greater detail about his welcome. Christina also spoke about the return voyage in her article of 18 January 1930. A good visual idea of their voyage out, and a tourist's impression

---

[15] Charles Maclean, *Island on the Edge of the World: The Story of St Kilda* (Canongate, 1972, 1992 edn), 153–5.
[16] Hutchinson, *St Kilda*, 145–7.
[17] Presumably Donald Ferguson, born 1880 later to become the Rev. Donald Ferguson.

of Hirta at that time, might be seen in a photographic album dating to that year of a voyage of the *Hebrides*, published by Campbell McCutcheon.[18]

In 1916 Christina and Robert had their first child Janet, or 'Jenny', Chalmers. In an echo of the horrific infant mortality on St Kilda, in January 1918 Christina gave birth to another daughter Nora, who tragically died only three months later. Misery would return the following year, when another daughter, Violet, died on 29 May 1919 aged only three weeks. Nora and Violet's burial plot in the Western Necropolis would later hold the bodies of Christina's sister Mary Gillies, and Mary's baby Annie.[19] Another son was born in 1920, Robert, then another, James Ramsay MacDonald, in 1924 (who also died in 1926). James was buried at St Kentigern's Churchyard, Stonehouse. Finally, two further sons, Donald and David, were born in 1924 and 1926 respectively.

We know relatively little of the family through the 1920s, although Robert is noted in the newspapers as part of the Stonehouse Silver Band, and was bandmaster from at least 1924 until resigning in February 1927. He was conductor for a time in 1925 at least.[20]

Back on St Kilda Christina's mother Marion died of heart failure on 10 June 1921. Presumably Christina would have travelled out to the island for the funeral. Her brother, Donald IV, had found work in 1916, during the First World War, as a lookout for the Royal Navy on Mullach Mor, for which he was paid two shillings a day. Sometime after the war, presumably between 1920 and 1924,

---

[18] Campbell McCutcheon, *St Kilda: A Journey to the End of the World* (Tempus, 2002).

[19] The grave location was unmarked and was identified in 2006 by Roger McStravick for Norman John Gillies (Mary was his mother) and David Chalmers (brother to Norah and Violet). Gillies and Chalmers commissioned a proper stone headstone for the spot. With thanks to John Gillies for passing on this story.

[20] *Dundee Courier*, 26 July 1924, p.2; *West Lothian Courier*, 3 July 1925; *Sunday Mail*, 13 February 1927, p.16.

he also left St Kilda, finding work in the Napier shipyard in Old Kilpatrick, alongside two other islanders.[21] This left Christina's sister Mary on the island. She had married John Gillies, and the couple took over number 10. In 1925, Mary gave birth to Norman John Gillies, who was named after Mary and Christina's two drowned brothers. Also remaining on the island was Christina's half-brother, the famous cragsman, Finlay MacQueen.[22]

When Christina left in 1903, the island had a more or less stable population, around 80. Little had changed by 1911, when the population was exactly 80 and in 1921 there were 73 individuals. After this point though, the number collapsed very quickly, and by 1928 there were only about 37 people left. The connections made in the war encouraged many of the young to move, while growing hardships on the island, exacerbated by lack of labour, created a cycle that forced many more of the young away. It was partly this drop in numbers and associated hardships that led to the evacuation of Hirta in 1930, which form the focus of Christina's writing.

---

[21] Gillies, *The Truth About St Kilda*, 11, 18.
[22] Quine, *St Kilda Portraits*, 34. Elisabeth Gifford, *The Last Families on St Kilda* (St Kilda Club, 2020); Calum MacDonald, *From Cleits to Castles: A St Kildan Looks Back* (Islands Book Trust, 2010, 2020 edn), 124.

1929–1930: Evacuation and Christina's Articles

The majority of the articles and photographs here were collected by Christina's eldest daughter, Jenny Chalmers. On Jenny's death, these passed to her brother David Chalmers of Penicuik. There was no note on the articles of the place of publication, although all have been subsequently identified. Further articles by Christina, and her husband Robert Chalmers, have been added. This book has arranged these in largely chronological order. Among the articles Jenny collected are other clippings relating to the fortunes and evacuation of St Kilda. These have been omitted here, although these were likely what Christina was reacting to in her articles, often with great frustration.

The dwindling population of St Kilda had become critical in the 1920s, as the exodus of young people after the First World War meant the necessary labours needed to sustain life could not be carried out. However, it is not immediately obvious what prompted Christina to start writing at the end of 1929. Some newspaper reports earlier in the year noted the dwindling population of the island, such as the *Evening Telegraph* of 27 May 1929, which commented on two deaths over the winter. In July the minister, John MacLeod left and was replaced by Dugald Munro, an event which really emphasised to the press the meagre population.[23] However, it was still thought that evacuation would

---

[23] *Fleetwood Chronicle*, 12 July 1929.

not be effected for some time.[24] More sustained worries about the island, and suggestions about abandonment, would not start until mid-December, by which time Christina had already started her *Hamilton Advertiser* series.[25]

Things came to a head in February 1930, when Christina's sister Mary Gillies suffered a difficult pregnancy. The resident nurse, Williamina Barclay, summoned Dr Alexander Shearer from the mainland, who took Mary to Stobhill hospital in Glasgow. Mary and her husband John left their 5-year-old son Norman John on the quayside in the care of his grandmother Annie. Mary would never see him again. In Glasgow, Mary was attended by her sister Christina, but died, along with her baby Annie, on 26 May 1930. Unable to send her body back to St Kilda, as was apparently Mary's last wish, she and her baby were buried in the plot of Christina's two infant babies in Glasgow's Western Necropolis. Newspaper reports of this unfolding tragedy have been inserted between Christina's articles. The death of her sister was the context in which Christina wrote the subsequent articles: in grief and facing the prospect that life on her home island was about to collapse. The crisis probably prompted Christina's run of articles in the *Dundee People's Journal* between May and June 1930.

On 10 May 1930 the remaining St Kildans wrote to William Adamson the Secretary of State for Scotland, seeking assistance to leave the island and 'find homes and occupations on the mainland'. This had been initiated by Nurse Barclay. Christina is distinctly cold about Barclay in her letters to the *Oban Times*. The issue was delegated to Tom Johnston, Under Secretary of State for Scotland, who went to St Kilda on 12 June 1930 and started making arrangements for evacuation. As evacuation came to be seen as inevitable to the outside world, Christina, and her

---

[24] *Sheffield Daily Telegraph*, 12 June 1929; *Port-Glasgow Express*, 12 June 1929; *The Tamworth Herald*, 16 June 1929.
[25] E.g., *Cleveland Standard*, 21 December 1929.

EVACUATION AND CHRISTINA'S ARTICLES

husband Robert, continued to write articles for the *Daily Express*, the *Oban Times, Hamilton Advertiser* and *Daily Record*.

Christina's articles, culminating most forcefully in the *Oban Times* of July 1930, reflected on the history and decline of the island, but also sought, in vain, to stop the evacuation, and to heavily criticise its necessity. Despite the 'united desire' of the remaining residents to leave,[26] Christina was against the decision, blaming the government for not providing the islanders with enough support. In July, following her letter in the *Oban Times*, she received a letter from Seamus Clann Fhearguis, an aristocratic adventurer living in New York, detailing a plan to halt the evacuation. Nothing came of this scheme and it is unclear whether Christina pursued it, or even what she thought about it.

By 19 July, the day Seamus wrote his battle plan, her husband Robert was in St Kilda, writing postcards from the island about the good time he and his father were having sightseeing and shooting puffins. They had arrived on 15 July. This was during the Glasgow Fair, so Robert would have had time off work, and the paper who likely commissioned the trip, the *Hamilton Advertiser*, had presumably paid his expenses. Robert took many photographs of his journey and penned articles for the paper about the trip. Christina probably remained in Glasgow looking after their children. Her sister's widower husband, John Gillies, her nephew Norman John Gillies (both living with John's mother in number 15), and her half-brother Finlay MacQueen were her main immediate family left on the island at this point. Robert recounts being

> present on the Island when the Government's documents relating to the disposal of the Islanders' flocks came to hand. They co-opted me as a member of their centuries-old Forum, and asked me to read over the terms. I did so, after which

---

[26] As reported by MacGregor, although Christina's half-brother Finlay seems to have been hesitant. Alasdair Alpin MacGregor, *A Last Voyage to St Kilda* (Cassell and Company, 1931), 226, 277.

they were translated into Gaelic for the benefit of the older members.

While the Chalmers were on Hirta, on 21 July, another islander, 22-year-old Mary Gillies, died. Robert took photographs of Mary's coffin being made by the men. The Chalmers were still on the island on 31 July, but Robert presumably had to leave soon after as he was called for jury duty (see Christina's letters to the Secretary of State for Scotland).[27]

Christina and her brother Donald both applied to the Secretary of State to be on the ship that would evacuate the last islanders. Both were denied this request and Christina's letter in reply is one of profound frustration. The tone in her article for the *Daily Record* of 29 August 1930 is ultimately one of grief and resignation. This grief is also present in her final, more measured, and most moving articles for the *Scots Magazine*, which end with her back in the cottage of Rachel MacCrimmon reliving a simple treasured memory of spinning wool.

* * *

An article in the *Oban Times* of 16 August 1930 suggested that Christina planned to write a book on St Kilda:

> ST KILDA AND ITS PEOPLE WILL LONG REMAIN A subject of interest. We have had books and articles on the appearance of the island, and on the ways of the inhabitants, but after all these have been but impressions of visitors. A book by a native of the island, by one who can interpret the thoughts and feelings of St Kildans, and give us their true character, will be of rare value. We understand that

---

[27] Robert presumably left before or at the same time journalist Alasdair Alpin MacGregor arrived on the *Hebrides* at an unspecified date in August, who penned an account of his journey and experiences in the final weeks of island life. MacGregor, *A Last Voyage to St Kilda*.

> such a work is being prepared by an isleswoman, Christina
> McDougall [Sic] MacQueen, whose name has become
> familiar to our readers as writer of the strong protest against
> the deportation, which appeared in a recent issue of the
> Oban Times. The real attitude of the people, especially of
> the older natives, towards their removal, which has not been
> grasped by outsiders, will be portrayed in the work.

We do not know what became of her effort, but it is hoped that by gathering her various writings and other materials, an impression of this lost work can at least be formed.

Christina's writings are important for three main reasons. First, they are an immediate body of writing in reaction to the evacuation by a former islander. An awful lot was written at the time by lots of people with strong opinions about the island, but all were the views of outsiders. Christina was a 'St Kildian'. Second, they are an important record of the social history of the island. Although many of the details have been recorded elsewhere, additional pieces of information are an important record of life on the island in the 1890s and 1900s, not least her experiences milking cows detailed in her article of 4 January 1930, or waulking with Rachel MacCrimmon. Third, Christina was the first and only female St Kildan to write about the islands, and this important perspective should not be under-appreciated.

Other islanders wrote about their time on the island, but these were mostly written many years after the evacuation, and from those of the generation following Christina. Neil Gillies, for example, was interviewed by David Quine: he was born in 1896 and left in 1919 to find work on the mainland, and started work at the Old Kilpatrick shipyard.[28] Donald John Gillies, born in 1901, left the island in 1924, and wrote when he was an older man an account in note form of his memories of St Kilda. He gives us further detail about the domestic arrangements on the

---

[28] Quine, *St Kilda Portraits*, 36–9.

island, especially in the period after Christina left.[29] Donald John's brother John was married to Christina's sister, Mary. Another, Calum MacDonald, born in 1908 (the year before Christina left), like Donald John, also left St Kilda in 1924 with his father. Calum wrote a more comprehensive autobiography of his whole life.[30] Lachlan MacDonald, born in 1906, was also interviewed by David Quine. Lachlan would stay on St Kilda up to the evacuation and recorded his schooling, work and life on the island, and even a holiday to Glasgow in 1927.[31] These memoirs provide useful counterpoints to Christina's writings, especially as the three have very different tones: Donald John and Calum were writing in the comfort of later life, whilst Christine's writing betrays, in real time, the rawness and pain around the tense context of the evacuation and her grief for her sister and island life more generally. David Quine also collected stories from the last generation of St Kildans, children at the time of the evacuation, including Flora Gillies (daughter of Annie Gillies, nee MacQueen, Christina's niece) born 1919; Norman John Gillies, born 22 May 1925; and Mary Cameron, daughter of the Minister from 1919 to 1926, which all add to the rich picture of the last years of island life.[32]

Alongside these islanders' memories, there are accounts by outsiders. The schoolmaster, George Murray kept a diary of his time there in the years 1886–87, when Christina was a baby. His diary gives a snapshot of island life at this point. Although Murray consciously tried to avoid island gossip and petty squabbles, his account gives a flavour of the social difficulties of living in such a small community. The diary also describes the men's activities, such as fowling and cultivation, and shows how he made an effort to

---

[29] Gillies, *The Truth About St Kilda*. Also see Quine, *St Kilda Portraits*, 39–52.
[30] MacDonald, *From Cleits to Castles*. Also see Quine, *St Kilda Portraits*, 148–84.
[31] Quine, *St Kilda Portraits*, 109–47.
[32] Quine, *St Kilda Portraits*, 31–2, 34; 185–95.

participate in these.[33] The diary of Alice MacLachlan, teacher on St Kilda 1906–09, is also published in Quine's *St Kilda Portraits* and covers Christina's last years on the island, including the tragic accident that saw two of Christina's brothers killed. MacLachlan seems to have had a happier time than Murray. She only mentions 'Christina McQuien' in passing once, and there is no mention of Christina leaving. MacLachlan left in May 1909, so presumably Christina left on a later vessel that year. MacLachlan makes a few mentions of Christina's father, including this wonderful portrait:

> Donald was in great form and was telling us heaps of stories about the island – pirates etc. I wished I had more Gaelic to understand better. He told us about men falling over the rocks at Soay – boys being stolen away from Boreray, and robbers coming to the island. His gestures were so funny and if any of the others dared to dispute anything he said he almost devoured them.[34]

Christina's recollections bridge the gap between Murray and MacLachlan on the one hand and the two Gillies and two MacDonalds on the other.

It is remarkable, given the vast literature about St Kilda, that Christina's voice has been largely ignored by historians. Tom Steel in 1975 makes two passing references to her writings, although he does not cite his sources. He strongly disagrees with Christina's assertion that the evacuation was 'the work of despairing Sassenachs', stating that it was an 'ignorant assertion'.[35] He completely ignores the original context of this line, following the frustration of being refused access to the ship carrying out the evacuation. The Sassenach quote he probably took from Francis

---

[33] Maureen Kerr, *George Murray*.

[34] Quine, *St Kilda Portraits*, 53–108.

[35] Tom Steel, *The Life and Death of St Kilda: The Moving Story of a Vanished Island Community* (Harper Press, 1975, 2011 edn), 47, 210.

Thompson's book of 1970, which was more sympathetic to her position.[36] Only Angela Gannon and George Geddes's 2015 book gives much attention to Christina, referring to her two letters to the Secretary of State for Scotland (source of the Sassenach quote) and her letters to the *Oban Times*.[37]

Among the family papers are two letter pages, with a note from Christina, written in red ink. It is unclear why she wrote it, but it serves as a fitting preface to the articles she published:

> Muinntir mo shine: muinntir Hirta! (People of my line, people of St Kilda)
>
> I have written these articles about far off lonely Hirta: far away and lonely myself, a stranger in the lowlands, longing always, and dreaming of days and folk that are no more.
>
> I have written to care my heart and that my children may know and know of the kindly race and distant isle from where their mother came. Never before has a daughter of Hirta written of the island home in an alien tongue. I am in hope that besides my children others may read of these fond memories, of a lonely isles and my people who lived so happy.
>
> Muinntir mo shine
>
> Faills dhauth es slainte mhath
>
> Christina McDonald McQueen

---

[36] Francis Thompson, *St Kilda and other Hebridean Outliers* (David & Charles, 1970), 120.

[37] Angela Gannon and George Geddes, *St Kilda: the Last and Outmost Isle* (Historic Environment Scotland, 2015, paperback edition 2016), 217.

St Kilda: My Island Home

PART I *Hamilton Advertiser*, 7 December 1929

ISLAND DEPOPULATION

In this, the first of a series of articles dealing with lonely St Kilda, the writer discusses the question of the island's depopulation. Subsequent articles will be of a reminiscent and historical character. The writer is a St Kilda lady, who, for a number of years, has been resident in the Middle Ward. – *Editor*

> A Time there was, e'er England's griefs began
> when every rood of ground maintained its man;
> for him light labour spread her wholesome store,
> just gave what life required, but gave no more;
> his best companions, innocence and health,
> and his best riches, ignorance of wealth
> —Goldsmith[38]

I suppose it is only those who can translate 'St Kilda' into the magic word of 'home' who will experience any feeling of regret at the announcement that its community of souls is threatened with extinction; that the island may ere long become merely a sanctuary for birds in the consequence of its gradual depopulation. The 'man in the street' will, I'm sure, remain quite passive when the last of the MacDonald's and MacQueens, the Gillieses, Fergusons and MacKinnons wave their farewells to the rock that for centuries gave shelter and succour to their forefathers.

---

[38] *The Deserted Village* by Oliver Goldsmith (1770).

This is only natural. The average mainlander only thinks about St Kilda as a home suitable for the fulmar, guillemot, gannet, kittiewake, puffin, and the numerous other species of sea birds that infest it. Perhaps, if I could remove sentiment from the scales of reason, I, too, would find them weighted on the side of the mainlander. For truly, within recent years, at least, St Kilda (or, to give it its proper name – Hirta) has become exceedingly difficult for the older people, and altogether impossible for the younger ones. Today it is like a house divided against itself. Its youth has fled, refusing to be longer shackled to its primitive environment. Old age is settled like a vulture upon its rocky steps. Hirta's Day has passed. Never since that remote time when the monks of Iona discovered it, and made of it a refuge, and a home, has the doom of its inhabitants seemed more imminent. The reason is simply that St Kilda could only exist in isolation. Now, however, the spirit of the age has caught it (that restless spirit so rampant everywhere), with the result that its young men and maidens desire to be stamped by that hallmark of modernity. Who shall blame them?

THE DAWN OF A NEW ERA

The birth of the 20th century found me, as it found my brothers and sisters in Hirta, gradually tasting of the fruits of civilization – and, believe me, to taste of the cherry was simply to swallow it whole.

The rapid development of science was then bringing the island ever nearer to the coast, so to speak, just as, on the mainland, it was bringing the hill nearer to the street, the country nearer to the town.

From the passing of the old sailing ship, the *Robert*,[39] sent out once a year by the MacLeod of MacLeod, to the coming of the

---

[39] Most likely the *Robert Hadden*, number 72415, a smack of 29 tons built at Dover and registered at Greenock in 1876 by John T.

tourist steamers, *Hebridean, Dunara Castle,* and *Hebrides,*[40] was like the passing from darkness into light. We all felt then that the 50 miles or so of treacherous ocean between our home and the islands of Harris and Uist had been shortened by more than half. 'How easy it would now be to go!' thought we, 'easier than even going to Boreray or Soay (islands in the vicinity) by our own little boat'. To my youthful companions and I the prospect opened up by such a change was not only alluring, but enchanting. (My question very much if a modern youth would be more thrilled by an aerial trip to the continent than we were then by their mere prospect of a Steamboat jaunt to Harris). Unlike Peter Pan, we could not grow up quickly enough.[41] We fretted, and sighed, and prayed for the day when the steamer would bear us off – away beyond the distant peaks of the mountains that, on clear days, seemed just an irregular pencil line on the horizon; away to the great cities where there were no peats to carry, and no wool to card, and spin.

YOUTHFUL RESOLUTIONS

Many a time, when turning the peats to dry on the slopes of Connachair or the Mullach Mohr (Peaks of the island, each over 1000 feet high) we would cease our task, and gather together in the Lee of a cleit (small conical built huts of loose stones in which the peats were stored through the winter), and there would hold a council, making our thousand resolutions to cut the bonds, and

---

MacKenzie of Dunvegan, Skye. She is mentioned several times by the schoolmaster George Murray, who was on Hirta 1886–87, was still active in 1890, but does not seem to have survived much longer. Crew List Project, https://crewlist.org.uk/data/vesselsnum/72415, accessed 4 November 2023; Kerr, *George Murray.*

[40] Dunara Castle began regular trips to St Kilda from 1877. Hutchinson, *St Kilda,* 187.

[41] J.M. Barrie's *Peter Pan* was first published in 1902, a year before Christina first left St Kilda.

go in search of that promised land. Those resolutions, however, were invariably swept aside by our elders assuring us that such great cities as Glasgow and London were only glorified examples of Sodom and Gomorrah. As year after year passed, bringing evermore tourists to the island, the assurances of our elders began to be discounted, and so, one bright summer morning I found myself on the deck of the SS *Hebrides*, calling out between the sobs "Soiridh Hirta!" ('Farewell St Kilda') As the island slowly sank astern – a stone into the sea.

I SPEND MY FIRST PENNY

That was five years prior to the outbreak of the Great War.[42] I had entered upon womanhood without seeing even such commonplace things as trees, horses, cycles, motor cars – in short, any of the things which go to make up the everyday existence of the mainland are. Further, I had yet to spend my first copper, and, believe me, I experienced no little difficulty in doing so.[43] Now, however, a much greater difficulty is that of getting sufficient of them to spend. For have I not made the acquaintance of the great mainland 'tax collector' – a personage who seems to be always itching for the last copper? My ignorance of money values in those early days appears to be not without some humour even to my own children, for when they plead with me for another copper for a lollipop, and I quietly yet sternly, remind them that I was 18 before I bought my first penny worth of sweets, they just burst out laughing, and chorus together 'oh, what a shame!' And who could resist such pleading?

---

[42] Namely 1909. Elsewhere she claims to have left in 1903 – see the *Daily Record* article of 29 August 1930. The mention further below about first buying sweets at the age of 18 would fit the 1903 date.

[43] Christina's experience as a young girl leaving the island is echoed in an article in the *Daily Mail* of 30 May 1928, which describes Rachel Annie Gillie's first trip to the mainland to Fleetwood and Blackpool from St Kilda. This is reproduced in Quine, *St Kilda Portraits*, 33.

THE CAUSE OF THE ISLAND'S DEPOPULATION

On that never-to-be-forgotten morning when I bade adieu to my island home as the first of St Kilda's woman to essay the great adventure, I left behind me a fairly happy and contented populous numbering, in all, 82.

Had anyone told me then that, within the period of a decade, it would have shrunk to less than half of that number, I should have felt disposed to disagree – and this, despite the fact that I was conscious of a desire on the part of the island's youth to see beyond the narrow confines of their home. But such is the somewhat startling fact today. This rapid decline of the population of the island is largely, if not wholly, the result of the late war, which settled the destiny of my island home just as effectively as it settled the destiny of kings and empires.

It was inevitable under the ever changing conditions which preceded the great worldwide catastrophe of 1914 that the population would gradually dwindle. Even the most pessimistic of the few St Kildians on the mainland, however, would scarcely have believed it would occur with such startling rapidity.

WAR-TIME SHIPPING AND ITS EFFECT

It is said that the first shot of the Great War 'shook the world'. In St Kilda – that for generations had been a world unto itself – that first shot may be said to have rocked it to its very foundation, completely transforming its social and economic life, and thrusting its inhabitants into the same channels of falsity as the whole world has since been floundering in. What it would have taken probably a century to accomplish under the ordinary conditions of peaceful penetration, and educational enlightenments, the war accomplished in a single stroke. Gone was its isolation!

The northern route to America, which had long been abandoned for that via the English Channel, had again to be resorted to, with the result that my island home found itself immediately in that new line of shipping. This was a great attraction not only to the Islanders, but (as events proved later) to the enemy.

GREAT CHANGES ARE EFFECTED

The immediate result of this changed shipping route to the American continent was that the ocean around St Kilda soon swarmed with German submarines. To combat this, a wireless station was erected and a naval unit quartered on the island. Telephone cables were run to its highest vantage points, and it's young men assigned the task of becoming hidden eyes for the patrols which kept a watch and ward upon our shipping. Wages were paid (a somewhat extraordinary procedure for St Kilda) and ample opportunity afforded of spending them through the medium of government vessels that were always coming and going.

My young sisters soon discarded the one piece dress (made for them by their fathers) for a modern blouse and skirt.[44] Soon, too, appeared the light stocking and the stylish shoe. Tastes thrived and multiplied in the new environment. With the young men cigarettes – that had hitherto been a rarity – became a common place. (In my young days I have known the men chew the clay of their old pipes for a taste of 'thick black').

Added to this, the sudden precipitation of the Islanders into the company of those who standards of life were as far removed from theirs as the poles, had an effect not dissimilar to that of a new toy to a child.

---

[44] Heathcote, writing in 1900, mentions 'if ... the women [might] undertake the tailoring of the islands, as well as their other duties, it is hoped they will succeed in making the children's clothes fit rather better than the men can do'. Heathcote, *St Kilda,* 78.

POST-WAR DIFFICULTIES

When the war terminated, and the gloss came off the toy, the young men of St Kilda found themselves unable to settle down to the old life. To go forward was difficult, but to go backwards – impossible! As in all other parts of the empire, this process of attempted adjustment to former social and economic standards was fraught with the greatest difficulty. There it was not a question of the withdrawal of a war bonus, or a little bit off the wages now and again. It was a wholesale cut. Everything went. As suddenly as they found venue and wonderful life, just as suddenly did they lose it. The smile of fortune soon turned to a frown of despair. The post war fates of my brothers and sisters will perhaps be better and more readily understood in the light of our own mainland experience. Years of concentration, but with a single aim (this successful prosecution of the war) had made us all, wherever located, somewhat indifferent to the growth of other factors that have since become not only the 'thorn of the politician', but the curse of the 'man in the street'. Out of the war years grew problems that the 'peace' has only magnified. 'St Kilda' is just one of them. A small one no doubt (just a stalk in the crop, or a drop in the bucket), yet large enough to have a lesson for all who care to think. However desirable it might be to us to return to 1914 standards, history teaches us that there can be no turning back. The march of civilisation must go on, irrespective of whether it lands us all in a wilderness. This, I suppose, explains why the youth of my island home are forsaking it, just as it also explains why the youth of the mainland are leaving the towns and villages in quest of a standard of living no worse (however better) than the post war years have accustomed them to.

REFLECTIONS

Everything considered, I ought to be thankful that the children of Hirta are leaving the island, and yet I am sad; Sad because I know that many of them will be disillusioned, and after a little while will sigh for the peace and quiet of home. It will then be too late. The island will have passed to the birds, and they to the ever growing army of the discontented. I am also sad, too, at the prospect of no one to welcome me home. To be unable to sing 'Chi mi na Mor-bheanna' ('the Mist Covered Mountains of Home')[45] as the vessel swings through the Sound of Harris is a punishment that a Gael, and least, will be able to understand. Many a time have I stood clutching the vessel's rail, and peering into the night for a sight of towering Boreray – an island some three miles out from home. On such occasions I would be crooning over and over again to myself the lines of the old song –

'O, chi chi mi na Mor-bheanna;
O, chi, chi, mi na Corr-bheanna;
O, chi, chi mi na Coir-each,
An chi mi na sgoran fo cheo –'

('Hoo, O! soon shall I see them, O,
Hee, O! see them O, see them, O,
Ho-ro! Soon shall I see them –
The mist-covered mountains of home.')

Now, however, it would appear that I am to be fated to find that the porky little puffin of the rocks has been laying and hatching out its solitary egg beneath the stones which mark the last resting place of my sires.

Can you wonder at my sadness?

---

[45] This song was composed by John Cameron/Iain Camshroin in 1856.

PART II *Hamilton Advertiser*, 14 December 1929

THE PLAGUE OF 1729, AND THE TRAGEDY OF 'STAC-AN-ARMIN'[46]

Only once in the history of my island home has the population been lower than the thirty-eight at which it stands today. That was exactly two hundred years ago (1729), when a plague of smallpox swept it, taking terrible toll of its hundred and eighty inhabitants, and leaving only a group of eighteen children and one grown male to mourn the tragic passing of their loved ones. Never before, or since, has a tragedy of such appalling magnitude been enacted. It is, by far, the most frightful and poignant chapter in the history of the island – a history that abounds in dark pages, the full details of which have seldom got beyond the circle of home.

As a little girl I have sat by the island peat fires, shivering in their warm glow as one or other of the old folks retold the story of 1729. On such occasions the wheels[47] would be still, carding pins lying idle, and from the roof beam the loom hanging listless and unattended. For maybe it was old 'Rachel'—the last of the MacCrimmons[48]—who was telling us of that awful battle with death. And when Rachel spoke, or sung at our peat-fire 'ceilidh', we were always close to her skirts. For och! but Rachel had a way with her – and what a memory, too! She could, for instance, tell all the names of the youthful survivors of the plague of 1729, how the plague came, and at what season of the year. All this, and

---

[46] It was actually 1727, see the introduction.
[47] Spinning wheels.
[48] See Christina's article on her for the *Scots Magazine*.

more, has the old Caillach[49] told me, while the crusies[50] spluttered from their rusty nails, and the winds outside made mournful music as they sighed round my island home. But Rachel is gone now. She sleeps in the little God's acre under Connachair beside her sires the last of St Kilda's MacCrimmons! But let me tell you all I know concerning the smallpox epidemic of 1729 ...

I have read of the Plague of London of that awful period in 1348 when the narrow and deserted streets of the (now) great Metropolis echoed to the clank of the common hearse, or were made hideous by the "call" of the bellmen – "Bring out your dead! Bring out your dead."

The picture of London then, in the grip of its raging pestilence, is, indeed, a dark and gloomy one. It is bright, however, in comparison with the picture of that lonely island tragedy of two hundred years ago, when the dying had to help to dig their own graves: when little children, fast in the grip of the disease, started from their beds to scrape the earth over the still warm bodies of their fathers and mothers; when every family had its own little cemetery but a few steps from its cottage door. Death moved swiftly amongst the people of St Kilda then. For them there was no escape. Unlike the people of London during the scourge of 1348, they could not flee from the pestilence. Some thirty leagues of treacherous ocean separated them from the islands of Uist and Harris, the nearest points to which, had they been able, they might have flown for safety. But fate was against them. The excessive virility of the disease, and the speed with which it assailed them, rendered every one of the inhabitants powerless in the face of possible escape. Even though a crew had been found to make the journey to Harris; the chances are

---

[49] Old woman.
[50] An open iron lamp in which fulmar oil would be burned. An example of one of these from Hirta is apparently among the collections of Dunvegan. The surviving examples were sold off as souvenirs in the last days before the evacuation. Harman, *An Isle Called Hirte*, 175; MacGregor, *A Last Voyage to St Kilda*, 164, 279.

they never would have reached it. Death had already marked them down. Their haven was to be the grave, not Harris. Truly it was a black day for St Kilda then. As an instance of the rapidity with which the disease assailed them, the following story will show:–

HOW THE PLAGUE CAME

According to historians (and in agreement with island tradition) the epidemic broke out immediately after the departure of the proprietors' vessel on or about the 12th of August, 1729, although the date and month of the year is not definitely stated by historians, we believe that it was in mid-August, and for certain well-defined reasons. These will become clear as I proceed. Apparently the proprietors' vessel made two calls that year – the first one in May, the second and tragic one in August. In those days St Kilda had a fairly large export of tweed, feathers, oil, and dried fish, people apparently believing then in the medicinal value of sea-birds' oil, and the physical comforts of a feather bed. Today, however, tastes have changed, and feather-beds are just about as obsolete as feather boas. If modern hygienics has wounded our faith in the one, fashion has killed the other which might be said to be a good thing for everybody concerned, save the people of my island home, whose only export now is tweed. In my young days fish could be had in abundance. But now, alas! Trawlers have scraped and scraped for years past over our once wonderful spawning beds until there is scarcely anything left in the sea around the island, save sharks and seals the former being at times very numerous in east or Village Bay, the latter on the rocks of the narrow channel between the main island and Soay.

On that memorable May morning of 1729, however, a very considerable cargo of island produce must have been taken on board the taxman's[51] 'Birlyn' or 'Galley', for it was agreed that a

---

[51] Taksman, or factor, the agent of the island's owners, the MacLeods of Dunvegan.

party of four natives should accompany the boat to Harris where, for the intervening three months, they would busy themselves in getting all their merchandise exchanged for the things the islanders required.

Towards the close of their holiday one of the party died, and, in ignorance that his death was the result of smallpox, his comrades gathered together all his belongings, and on the return of the proprietors' vessel had them taken home to the island. Thus were the people of St Kilda brought into contact with the fell scourge. Within a remarkably short period it was raging, making it impossible for the sole grown-up survivor to dig the necessary amount of graves. In this gloomy occupation he was engaged from dawn till dusk. Perhaps readers will be better able to grasp the significance of the high rate of mortality by considering it with the black plague of London in 1348. Then the death-rate (according to Professor Thorald Rogers and De Gibbons[52]) was 33 per cent, or one in every three of London's population. In St Kilda, however, it was 90 per cent, or only one in every ten escaping with their lives. How the lone male survivor won through is one of those mysteries which must be assigned to fate. For, like the rest of the natives then, he was totally unacquainted with the nature of the disease, or the remedies which might have been employed as a precaution against it. His family all perished. He found another family in the eighteen little orphans, whose sad hearts he contrived to heal, and whose bodies he clothed and nourished; watching and caring for them throughout the years till, when of age, he gave them the inheritance that was their fathers. It is difficult to conceive a more tragic picture than that of this lone islesman with his little flock, praying every hour for the coming of a sail; ever gazing seawards for the boat that never came; lighting fires

---

[52] James Edwin Thorold Rogers, 1823–90, wrote various works on English history. The work referred to here is possibly *A History of Agriculture and Prices in England*, vol. 1 (Oxford, 1866). Gibbons is possible Alfred W. Gibbons.

on the point of Oiseval, Bi, Mullach Mor and Connachair in the hope that their signals would be seen and answered. Not, however, until the following May, when the taxman called again for his croft rents, were they discovered, and then but a heart-broken group on the rocky shore.

THE TRAGEDY OF STAC-AN-ARMIN

To acquire a fuller knowledge of the horror of this epidemic of 1729, and to bear out my earlier statement as to the extraordinary speed with which the disease decimated the islanders, let us now consider the following:– On that fateful August morning, when the proprietors' vessel brought the plague to the island, a party of six men and a like number of boys had been despatched to Stac-an-Armin for the autumn fowling. Stac-an-Armin is a bare, gaunt rock jutting church-steeple-wise out of the sea to a height of fully 600 feet. It is the highest pyramidical rock in the British Isles, and, like all of the stacks in the St Kilda group, is exceedingly difficult to effect a landing upon. A favourite nesting place for the fulmar, petrel, gannet and solan goose, these birds lay their eggs and hatch out their young on the exposed ledges of its precipitous sides. As there is no anchorage at Stac-an-Armin, it is necessary when on a fowling expedition to have an independent crew, whose duty it is to see the fowlers safely landed, together with the ropes for the perilous undertaking and provisions for their stay. This accomplished, the boat returns to Village Bay, where it is drawn up to await the expiry of the time agreed upon by the fowlers. After the lapse of a few days the youthful crew will again put to sea. Soon they are at Stac-an-Armin bringing off the fowlers, their gear, and their harvest of birds.

That memorable expedition of 1729, however, the crew of boys failed to return, which is proof that they all fell victims to the plague. It also proves that, in the interval covering their departure to and return from Stac-an-Armin, the proprietors' vessel must have called at St Kilda. Had it called prior to their departure, then the story of Stac-an-Armin and its six tortured souls would never have been written. For they, too, would have caught the germs and perished. But they lived – lived while death made of their homes a shambles. All through the winter they wrestled with starvation on that lonely rook of the sea. Their faith that God would hear and answer their prayers sustained them amid all their sorrows – and they had a surfeit. For food they had the birds of the rocks and the fish of the sea, the latter being caught by a primitive hook. They left it on record that, during their nine months incarceration, on Stac-an-Armin, the sea simply boiled with fish, proving (if mankind has any doubt) that "He who feeds the ravens fed Hirta's fowlers, too!" Their garments, long since torn to shreds by the jagged edges of the rocks, were replaced by others from the skins of fowls.

When we add to the horror of their situation the suspense in which they were held at receiving no intelligence from their loved ones on the main island, it is surely a marvel that they were able to live through it. From August till the following May when relieved by the proprietors' vessel, those six St Kilda natives had endured the maximum of physical and mental torture on that awful stack of the sea. Throughout the winter it would be drenched by the spray of mighty breakers and swept by Atlantic gales. It is, indeed, a terrifying picture. And what of their home-coming? Of the 174 whom they left in the flush of health, they found, only a handful of children – and amongst them none of their own! ...

Can you wonder how that on winter evenings at our peat-fire 'Ceilidhs' I used to sit close to the skirts of the old 'Caillach'[53] trembling, seeming to hear in the pauses of her narrative, the spirit voices of the lonely fowlers of Stac-an-Armin?

---

[53] Old woman.

PART III *Hamilton Advertiser*, 21 December 1929

ON THE ORIGIN OF THE NAME, AND AN ISLAND DESCRIPTION

The name 'St Kilda' has but little significance to a native. It is Anglo-Saxon; and what is perhaps, more important, is a misnomer. Ever since leaving home the name has had a sort of fascination for me; largely, I suppose, because most people imagine it applies only to the island of my birth. Such is not the case. 'St Kilda' does not signify one island, but a trio of islands and numerous stacks, the principal of which is 'Hirta' – this latter according to Kenneth MacAulay,[54] being probably a contraction of the Latin etymon, 'Herthus', which means 'Mother Earth'. 'St Kilda' is a 'group name', applying equally to the various stacks, or pyramidical rooks, in the vicinity. Let me explain. The name (as far as I can gather) was first applied to the group early in the seventeenth century by one Peter Goas, a chart maker of Amsterdam. Prior to this date historians when referring to the main island, do so by the name of 'Hirta'. Martin Martin, who visited it in 1697, refers (in the course of a historical survey of the island) to a charter of King Robert II conferring 'Hirta' and the other islands of the group, upon his son, Reginald.[55]

HOW THE CHANGE WAS EFFECTED

Since the Anglo-Saxon name 'St Kilda' appears for the first time on the sea map, or chart, prepared by the Dutchman, Peter Goas, it is only natural to assume that he was responsible for the change. He charted the ocean lying between Ireland and

---

[54] Kenneth Macaulay, *The History of St Kilda* (1759).
[55] Martin Martin, *A Late Voyage to St Kilda* (1698).

Zeeland. To perform this very useful service to the seafarers of his day, Peter Goas and his mariners must have sailed in and out of the group, probably landing on Hirta, and making friends with the islanders. The island (now referred to as St Kilda) was certainly inhabited then, for Martin found, towards the close of the same century, a very large population, the largest it has ever been. Further, existing evidences in the form of crude underground dwellings seem to suggest a very early occupation, dating back to the first or second century. Since the chart maker of Amsterdam found a new name for the group, he must have received it from the natives. If such be the case, then the name was either wrongly given, or, what is equally significant, wrongly interpreted. The language spoken by the natives then (as now) was Gaelic, and this would most certainly prove a stumbling block to the Dutchman and his crew.

ST KILDA OR ST HILDA—WHICH?

It is said by historians (subsequent to the Dutchman's period) that the name 'St Kilda' is derived from a religious well in the island, which bears the name of 'St Kilder', or, as we say in Gaelic, 'Tobar Childa'. How the well came to have such an appellation bestowed upon it is a mystery; a mystery no less puzzling than the saint whose name it bears, and whose memory it purports to perpetuate. A glance at the calendar of those early disciples of the Christian faith will suffice to convince that no such 'Saint Kilder' ever existed. The nearest approach to the name, phonetically at least, is that of Saint Hilda – the female saint who founded the Abbey of Whitby, in Durham and, whom tradition asserts, performed many miracles. The likeness between the two names is so pronounced that, like the Rev. Kenneth MacAulay, I am tempted to believe the well in question was actually dedicated to the saintly Lady of Durham – perhaps by a party of her immediate followers or, some time later, by a crew of southern sailors.[56] The custom of naming wells after favourite saints was much in evidence amongst the ancients. It is therefore quite within the bounds of reason to imagine such a party landing on the island, say, in search of water, and, finding it in abundance, to bestow upon it (the well) the name of their patron saint. Such then is the only explanation I can offer for the origin of the Anglo-Saxon name, 'St Kilda', by which the island is known today.

THE ISLAND'S CONTOUR – A CONTRAST

Since commencing these articles dealing with my island home, I have been casting about for some suitable object in the county by which to illustrate the form or contour of the island. I cannot say that I have been successful. There is a point, however, between the parishes of Stonehouse and Sandford from which one may gaze south-eastward to the dominant hill of Tinto, and westward to the equally pronounced mass of Loudon Hill. Seen from this vantage point, both hills bear, at least, a slight resemblance to the islands of 'Hirta' and 'Soay' respectively. On a May morning, when the valleys are filled with mist and the peak and shoulders of Tinto ride above it, the resemblance may be said to be striking. The contour of Tinto changes, however, as the mists dispel, just as all stationary objects at sea change as the vessel approaches. Some ten leagues or so south-east of St Kilda one might readily associate its highest peak (that of Mount Connachair, 1,390 feet) with that of our south Lanark landmark. As you sail closer, however, the form of the island will change. The peak of Connachair will gradually disappear, giving place to a frightfully steep and rocky mass, upon which at first you will think it impossible to land. Everywhere it

---

[56] 'Tobar Childa' actually means 'the well' in Gaelic and Norse respectively. Hutchison, *St Kilda*, 41. MacAulay actually dismissed his own idea of an association with Saint Hilda. Harman, *An Isle Called Hirte*, 43.

seems just a perpendicular wall of rock. Soon, however, your eye will discern a break in the cliffs, and, in sailing closer, this will gradually resolve itself into a loch. Entering it, between points of 'Oiseval' and 'Dun', you will get another and better view of Mount Connachair, with the sixteen little whitewashed dwellings lying crescent-shaped at its base. This is the village of Hirta. By the time the skipper has shouted "let go for'ard!" and the anchor cable has shot overboard with a rattle and a clank, you will have counted all the dwellings from the little church on the right to the MacDonald's cottage on the extreme left.

POSTAL FACILITIES

As there is no harbour, your vessel daren't go too close inshore. So you will remain in the middle of the loch, swinging on your anchor, waiting and wondering what next. You won't have long to wait. Out from the rocks the island boat will shoot, manned by a crew long accustomed to the swinging of an oar. It will soon glide under your lea quarter. You will be invited to descend the rope ladder and board it – which you will do if you would know St Kilda and its people. Perhaps you will wet your feet on landing, but a walk along Main Street and a climb to the top of Connachair will be ample compensation for such an inconvenience. If you smoke, don't leave your tobacco! If you have a sweet tooth, let me tell you the children of Hirta have a sweeter! There are no shops in the village and no tarmacadam on its single street. You will therefore enjoy the novelty of walking where, instead of looking at the shops, you will have to look to your feet. In the post office (for contrary to popular belief there is such an institution) you will buy Postcard views of the island.[57] These you will stamp and post in the usual way, and not, as some ill-informed

---

[57] The Post Office on Hirta was established in September 1899. Rev. Fiddes was the first postmaster, then Neil Ferguson succeeded in 1905 and served to 1930. Spirited descriptions of scenes at the post office in

people suggest, by placing them in an oilskin wrapper, enclosing the same in a wooden float attached to a sheep's bladder whereon the words, 'St Kilda Mail, Please Open!' have been painted, and then cast into the sea. Such a method of communicating with the mainland is ancient. It belongs to the days when only one regular vessel called – that of the tax man.[58] Some six years ago I requested my brother to send me a note in such a way, as my husband was curious to see how long it would take. According to instructions the letter was duly posted. I received it nine months later. It had simply drifted about the ocean, eventually being picked up by a trawler skipper between St Kilda and Iceland, and later posted to me from Fleetwood.

LADY GRANGE'S DWELLING

As you pass along the village enroute for the pathway that will lead you to the top of Connachair, you will, no doubt, be on the lookout for Lady Grange's dwelling. You will find it just opposite the tenth cottage – the one in which I was born.[59] The 'woman of sorrow'—Lady Grange—was wife to James Erskine of Grange, a brother of John, Earl of Mar, who (as all familiar with Jacobite history know) acquired some little notoriety for the part he played in the rising of 1715. Whatever bad points 'Bobbing John' may have had, his brother James easily eclipsed them. For no amount of whitewash will ever obscure the dark blot which the inhuman treatment of his wife has left upon his character. In the year 1734

---

its final days are recounted by MacGregor. Maclean, *Island on the Edge of the World*, 153; MacGregor, *A Last Voyage to St Kilda*, 217, 283–4.

[58] The 'mailboats' were actually thought up by John Sands, a frequent visitor to the islands, in 1877, and developed by the islanders. Maclean, *Island on the Edge of the World*, 150–2.

[59] Norman Heathcote, writing in 1900, thought her dwelling to have been demolished. It survives, however, albeit altered, but is identified now as cleit 85. Heathcote, *St Kilda*, 27; Andrew Fleming, *St Kilda and the Wider World* (Windgather Books, 2005, reprint 2016), 135.

he had his wife seized by a party of lawless rogues: bound hand and foot upon a Highland sheltie;[60] driven through the almost impassable glens to the coast; and, finally, shipped in a vessel to St Kilda. For eight weary years she dwelt with my forefathers, while her friends on the mainland mourned her as dead. It isn't much to look at, this one-time prison home of the 'lady of sorrow'; she who, during her years of incarceration, used to weep on the shore when the first bird, the sheerwater, brought its tidings of spring. The old house, with its irregular walls of unhewn boulders and its roof covered with turf, is now used as a storing place for peats. As you stand surveying this monument to a husband's callous indifference, you may resurrect again the picture of James Erskine's foul crew driving the defenceless woman to this lowly shack, and, with curses and threats, abandoning her to the care of strangers. If the truth were known, more than her husband were implicated in this crime. What about MacLeod's taxman who called, once at least, every summer for the croft rents? He was bound to be acquainted of the lady's plight. Was he in the pay of her husband? Such thoughts as these may occupy your mind as you toil up the steep slopes of Connachair.

THE CLIFFS OF CONNACHAIR

When you have won to the summit, all thoughts of Lady Grange's ordeal will have passed. A feeling of delight, not unmixed with wonderment and awe, will have taken possession of you. For, instead of finding the other side of the mountain a gradual descent to the sea, you will stop short on the edge of the highest cliff in the British Isles. You will be tempted to give credence to the legend that a giant of the past split the mountain with a mighty sword, one half falling out to lose itself in the ocean far below. If you are nervous, you will have crawled the last few yards. Shuddering now, you will peer down the one thousand two hundred feet of

---

[60] Shetland Pony.

cliff, on the ledges of which the fulmar or guillemot may be sitting on their eggs, or, if it be the month of August, endeavouring to teach their young ones how to fly.

PART IV *Hamilton Advertiser*, 28 December 1929

REMINISCENCES

Last week I gave you a description of the main island of the group. If I remember aright, this was broken off when we had won to the island's highest peak (Mount Connachair) and discovered that the back of it was simply a wall of rock some 1,200 feet high. The ledges which intersect this stupendous cliff are the favourite haunt of the fulmar, guillemot and sheerwater. Here, too, sea parrots (or puffins) reside in great numbers. The puffin is, in certain respects, well termed a sea parrot, for its bill is crooked and its eye very prominent – this latter being a bright red with a white circle round it. Its plumage is black and white, the former on its upper parts, the latter on the breast and under the wings. Seen at close quarters, the puffin is a decidedly intriguing little fellow. When you get too close to him, however, he will either take to flight or waddle on his bright yellow webbed feet further along the ledge, inclining his head this way and that, as much to say – "Who are you, and what do you want?" You will find this pawky little bird quite at home in a hole under a boulder, or in a small burrow scraped on the hillside. There is a part of the adjacent island of Soay, where the hillside is so riddled with these puffin holes that you find it quite impossible to walk without stepping on them. The egg of the puffin or sea parrot is much the same in size and colour as that of the farmyard hen, and is remarkably large for the size of the bird. This feature is peculiar to most sea fowl. The puffin can be very tricky and treacherous, and if you are unacquainted with his ways, is sure to catch you napping. I shall never forget the first occasion on which my husband tried to catch one. Very gingerly he inserted his hand into the cavity under the stone, but in a more definite and decided manner withdrew it, the forefinger bearing a wound from which the blood trickled. I laughed heartily, and passed him my handkerchief. Well I knew the puffin. He didn't, of course, and, well, that made all the difference.

CANINE FELICITY

Long ago we trained dogs to the work of Puffin catching, some of them being exceedingly clever. When a little girl at home, my father had such a dog – a dear little thing, though it was only a mongrel. It was so crossed in breed that an expert would have experienced difficulty in determining what it came from. But it was intelligent. Exceedingly so. All father needed to say to it was "Puffin's, Teddy!" (this, of course, in Gaelic, for we didn't believe then in teaching our dogs English) and instantly he was out the door and scampering away to the cliff tops. A little later we would see him come down the hillside with one or two puffins in his mouth. And woe betide anyone who would have dared to interfere with him! Teddy simply refused to drop the birds, unless at my father's feet. For this he was generally rewarded with much kindly stroking, and (if there were any about) a nice, juicy, mutton bone. This he invariably carried to the ash rim of the peat fire, where he lay contentedly worrying it, while the other dogs looked on with envy.[61]

---

[61] MacGregor notes that the St Kildan dogs were a type of mongrel collie, of no use at rounding up sheep, but very good at catching and holding down individual sheep. MacGregor, *A Last Voyage to St Kilda*, 170.

A FISHY TALE

The feathers of the puffin – at least the softer breast feathers – used to be much in demand. Now, however, there is no sale for feathers of any kind. It is changed days for the folks of Hirta. Upwards of thirty years ago I used to help in the plucking of the puffin harvest, singing as the heap of downy feathers grew and grew until I stood in the midst of them looking, I suppose, like a character from some weird novel. The flesh of this pawky little sea parrot (like that of the fulmar) is very tasty. To the more exacting palate of the mainlander, however, it might seem just a little bit fishy, although, mind you, food of a distinctly fishy character is not unusual on the mainlander's table. After all, I prefer fresh food which tastes fishy to the other variety which distinctly lacks it. Despite all that has been written to the contrary, the modern St Kildian is perhaps just as careful in his choice of fresh victuals (although these are distinctly limited) as the most exacting mainlander is. I well remember an old retired major[62], who used to spend his summers on the island, developing an extraordinary regard for the flesh of our cliff birds – particularly the fulmar and puffin. At first he refused to eat them politely. If pressed, he scorned them—generally—to the accompaniment of a good long string of Sassenach curse. One day, however, the major was exceedingly hungry and old Mr Fiddes, the missionary (with whom he stayed) was very short of mainland victuals – this as a result of a storm which compelled the mail boat to return to Glasgow without landing the stores. Mr Fiddes therefore asked Kate (his help) to cook him some fulmars. This she did in an excellent manner by roasting them over the peat flame. When the major came in to dinner he confessed that the smell was distinctly appetising, but when the plateful of fulmar was passed to him he demurred. 'Old Angus' (for so we called our dominie-divine)

---

[62] Possibly Major Niel MacLeod, 1825–98, Royal Artillery, a veteran of the Crimean War. *Dundee Evening Telegraph*, 5 December 1898.

informed him, however, that that was all he had till the boat came, and that, if he would but put aside his lowland antipathy and get to grips with them, he would be sure to find them good and satisfying. Awhile he played with his plate until hunger conquered. Then he set to in earnest. Succeeding summers found the major bringing a markedly lighter box of provisions to the island. The last time I saw him was when he was coming home to the manse from Carn Mor (a point directly opposite Connachair on the other side of the island) with his dinner of birds hanging round his neck like a feather boa.

ST KILDA'S FIRST HAM-AND-EGG BREAKFAST

This story of the major and his ultimate passion for roasted fulmars leads me on to another in which the Rev. Angus Fiddes again figures. Just as our old minister and schoolmaster converted the Sassenach major to a just appreciation of our somewhat fishy-tasted victuals, so also did he convert us to an equally just appreciation of that Sassenach breakfast dish which has formed an almost indissoluble partnership with eggs, i.e., ham. When first we saw it with its coat on we thought it was very fishy indeed. It was the Rev. Angus Fiddes who first introduced this mainland delicacy to the breakfast tables of Hirta. Of course, it was just a stroke of luck, and happened like this. Early one morning (almost forty years ago) a large vessel hove in sight, bearing on a course which suggested to us that the island was its objective. We were right, for it slowed down about two miles off and gradually approached the entrance to Loch Hirta, or Village Bay. From this point it called to us, with a few blasts from its siren, to send out a boat. We did so, and were delighted to see it return, literally packed with provisions and with scarcely an inch of freeboard. There was meal and flour, sugar, tea, tobacco, tinned foods and – ham! Indeed, there were hams – one, at least, for every dwelling. But we didn't know what hams were, so, after equally distributing the provisions, it was decided to commit the incongruous chunks of pig into the sea. It was then that the old dominie-divine came on the scene. He upbraided us for our stupidity, telling us that, with the accompaniment of eggs, ham formed the principal breakfast dish of the Sassenach. It all seemed strange to us, however. The end of it was that the minister took temporary possession of the hams, at the same time giving any of us who cared a hearty invitation to the manse at tea-time. We forgot all about the invitation, however, in the ordinary routine of village life. Towards evening we were reminded of his offer by a delicious smell floating up amongst the dwellings. Everybody immediately commenced sniffing and walking mansewards. A slice of it between a scone was enough to send everyone entitled careering for their ham and, at the same time, in quest of a frying pan. Alas, there was but one on the island – and the minister had it. So everybody went aborrowing. One dear old soul tried to overcome this difficulty by frying it on the girdle, but the grease trickled into the red peats, and a flame shot up to the riggin tree, giving the old soul such a fright, that she, too, had to fry her Sassenach breakfast on the minister's much-borrowed frying pan.

WHEN WE FIRST TASTED APPLES

It was about this same period that apples first made their appearance in the island. The skipper of an Aberdeen trawler brought them – a Captain Walker (I believe he is still living.)[63] He was a great friend of the islanders, and must have been amongst the first trawler skippers to make frequent voyages to our fishing

---

[63] A Captain Walker appears in the newspapers several times in relation to St Kilda. The *Dundee Evening Telegraph* of 5 November 1896 reported how Walker 'of the steam line fishing boat *Evening Star*' delivered to Aberdeen money collected by the St Kildans for suffering Armenians. The *Dundee Courier* of 1 May 1907 reported he had been arrested for not paying a fine for fishing around St Kilda in the vessel *Knowsie*.

beds. 'Twas a calm day in January, just prior to our celebration of the new year, when he steamed into the bay. Our new year, of course, was celebrated according to the old calendar – January 13. When any vessel called in my young days there was always a terrible commotion. So we were all at the rocks, as eager and anxious as a brood of chickens awaiting their pick. We knew he would bring us sweets – and we had a very pronounced weakness for them. On this occasion, however, Captain Walker not only brought sweets, but a large barrel of American apples. The barrel was opened under the supervision of the old minister. We expected it to contain biscuits – water biscuits. Judge of our surprise, and delight, when our eyes rested on what appeared at first to be painted toys – balls, or something of that sort. Every time I see an apple now I experience a strong desire to laugh outright. For, on that January afternoon, almost forty years ago, I received from Captain Walker that which I thought was but a something to play with, to throw up and catch again. Nor was I the only one present who thought the same. It is difficult to describe my feelings, however, when I saw old Angus Fiddes take two bites out of one. This was the signal for all to do likewise. Old and young immediately commenced an assault on the barrel. The new taste was devastating, so we ate, and ate, and continued eating till the barrel was emptied of its contents, and the skipper had put to sea. One can surely imagine the effect of an overdose of apples on those so much used to salted food! The result of it was that, while Captain Walker rode at anchor out-bye in the lea of Borrera, we were all experiencing what a mainlander today would pronounce as an unmistakable cruschen feeling.[64]

---

[64] This expression came from advertisements for Kruschen Salts, referring to a feeling of vitality.

A STRANGE ISLAND MALADY

The natives of my day and generation were much indebted indeed to old Angus Fiddes.[65] Not only did he labour for our souls' moral and spiritual salvation, but also for our material and physical wellbeing. In this latter field the most important was his successful effort to stamp out a strange malady that for years had taken its toll of the infants of Hirta. Just prior to my advent almost every child born on the island died at the eighth or tenth day from a form of lock-jaw.[66] Young wives, too, were generally regarded as having their doom sealed when carrying their first child. It was a frightful time. My own mother has told me how, with another isleswoman, she made the journey to Harris to be delivered of her first child, and after a year's absence returned to my father without it. The other woman's child survived. So serious had the position become that the old dominie-divine suspected all was not right with the maternity work of the native nurse, and decided that something ought to be done. Well, old Angus did it. He first tried to persuade the islanders to allow a nurse from the mainland to instruct them. When this failed he himself sailed for Glasgow, where he took a course in the work under a well-known professor, returning to the island later and instructing my Aunt Margaret[67] in the correct methods to be adopted. From that day onwards a marked improvement was noticeable. Young wives no longer regarded motherhood with fear and apprehension. A new light shone on love's path-way. The song, that for years had remained

---

[65] Christina remembers Fiddes fondly, although on the island near the end of his tenure there was growing dissatisfaction with him, partly due to his absences on the mainland. Hutchison, pp.263–5. For a comprehensive account of Fiddes tenure on the island, see Michael Robson, *St Kilda: Church, Visitors and 'Natives'* (Island Books Trust, 2005), especially part 8, chapters 2–4, especially pp.699–702.

[66] Fiddes arrived on the island in 1889, so the problem was very much there when Cristina was born in 1884.

[67] Margaret MacDonald 1839–1926, sister to Christina's mother.

unsung at the waulking of the tweed, was again on the lips of all. We praised God, and prayed for old Angus. Today he sleeps in a little churchyard somewhere in Easter Ross, his life's work accomplished, and sure of his reward.

PART V *Hamilton Advertiser*, 4 January 1930

AN ISLAND MILKING

> Morag is singin'
>   Doon the hill track,
> Morag is bringin'
>   Prettyfood back.
> Blithely she's liltin'.
>   Canty and free,
> For hame at the milkin'
>   Morag will be.

Upwards of thirty years ago I would be thinking it a long way from the village to Gleann Mor (1) [68] where, in summer, the cattle go to graze, and the lassies must go to the milking. Aye, and you would be thinking it a long way too, if, between dawning and gloaming, you had twice to make the journey with a milk pail and a peat bag slung upon your back. Maybe if you think of the distance in miles, it will seem short – for it is only one and a bit. Aye, but it will be up for one, and doon for the bit, which

---

[68] These notes are as they appear in the article as originally published. None of the others in this series has them.

makes it all the heavier for the steppin' of it. From the cottages strung round the base of Connachair, up to where the hill track tips the crest of Mullach Gael, is a stiff climb. Here you will be high above the sea; so high that, in looking downwards, you will be thinking some fairy has changed the village since you turned your back upon it. Smaller, and less regularly disposed, the houses will appear, with the smoke of their peat fires curling up against the green background of Connachair and looking just as an artist would paint them on his canvas. And you will be seeing the bay, too, as it never appeared to you before. For it will be under your eye—the full, graceful sweep of it—from Oiseval to Dun (2).

Up there on the crest of the hill, where the track dips over and into Gleann Mor, you will be wanting to tarry. Just there, where I, too often tarried – but it wouldn't be aye for the joy of it. Many a time I would be sitting there tired and leg-weary after my climb – so tired that I would be hoping "Prettyfoot" (3) was waiting for me just over the crest. Sometimes she wouldn't answer my call of "Crodh! Crodh!!" but go off in a huff to the bottom of the glen; away down to the sea on the other side of the island; away down past Tobar Nam Buaidh (4) and Tigh Na Banagaisgh (5). Och! but it would be a long way then to the milkin'! Maybe the other lassies would be laughing at me flyin' barefoot doon Gleann Mor, so that I would be angry with them, and with Prettyfoot forby. All the way down, the glen I'd be saying between the puffs: "Wait till I get ye! Wait till I get ye!!" But when I won to her side, instead of scolding her, I'd be stroking her dappled coat, syne singin' to her the old hillside milking song. "I hu o Leiginn"–

> M'endail fein an t-aghan caisfhionn,
> Chuirinn buarach air a chasan,
> Chuirinn buarach air a chasan–
> Buarach shioda thig a sasunn.
>   I hu o Leiginn!

Aye, and as I crooned it o'er, she'd just turn her head and look at me with eyes big with understanding–

> Come away my whitefoot pretty,
> You're whiles ready wi' yer fuitie,
> Bourach strang we'll hae tae get ye–
> Silken bourach frae the city,
>   Ee hoo the milkin'!

Maybe my singin' of it wouldn't please you. But it pleased prettyfoot-for she would just be kennin' what I meant, and, sooner than that I should be getting a rope to tether her with, she would be giving me all the milk she had. With the pail at my feet, and her head on my shoulder, I'd be saying to her, while her tail whisked this way and that–

> "Lang e'er tea was brocht frae China,
> Lang e'er man had tasted wine o,
> What put smeddum in oor kine o,
> What but milk like this o thine o,
>   Ee hoo the milkin'!"

* * *

Aye, it will be many years since I last heard the echo of my voice amongst the rocks of Gleann Mor. Many cattle have gone to Lochmaddy (6) market since then, and great are the changes that have taken place in the island of my birth. There will be few lassies now takin' the steep path to the milkin'. There will be fewer still. To the St Kildians of the next generation the hill track to Gleann Mor will only be seen in their dreams – just as I will be seeing it when night and its silence has wooed me to sleep.

THE EWE MILKIN – AN OLD CUSTOM

A St Kilda milking of thirty years ago and upwards included (at least for two months of the summer) the milking of the ewes as well as the cows. To milk the ewes it was necessary to separate the lambs from their mothers and fold them overnight in the turf huts on the hillsides. Here you were sure to find the mothers, at break o'day, with well filled udders, waiting on their young. This was aye, to me, a sad milkin'; for the milk, which ought to have gone to suckle the lambs, found its way, of course, into our pails. With the milk we make butter and cheese. In those days of few facilities for intercourse with the mainland, and when the population was more than double what it is today, necessity knew no law. To life, we had to smother sentiment. While there were lambs on the hillsides, there were also children in the village. From the month of May till the end of August-aye. And sometimes well into September—we would be going up and over into Gleann Mor twice a day. On the return journey we had not only to bring the milk, but a sack of peats as well. These we obtained from one or other of the little bee-hive structures which, made of loose stones and turf, and called "cleets", dot all the hillsides. Visitors to the island seem to take a great interest in them. They are everywhere. Each family owns so many and the natives refer to them by the family name, such as: MacDonald's cleet, Gillies' cleet, MacQueen's cleet, etc. In them the peats are stored after being dried. Since they are built of loose stones, it permits a current of air to be always passing through, thus keeping the peats in excellent condition for burning.

PRIMITIVE METHODS

On the way to the milking, then, we would be filling our peat bag at one of the cleets and leaving it convenient to the hill track. After the milking we would securely cover and fasten the pail. This we did by using a cover of sheepskin. We would fold it over the pail and tie with a piece of string, thereby making a lid which, though somewhat primitive, was certainly very serviceable. The pail thus fastened we would place in the sack amongst the peats and, swinging it on to our backs, would carry the lot down the hillside in much the same fashion as a fisherwoman carries her creel. While the summer milking lasted it was hard and strenuous work. There were two days of the week, however, when the journey to the glen never seemed so long. These were Sunday and Monday. On the former we had neither milk nor peat to carry home. To have done so would have been regarded as a very great sin.

A HILLSIDE DISH

Maybe you'll be wondering what we did with Sunday's milk since we didn't bring it home to the village? Well, we just left it till Monday – left it in pools of the little hill burn that empties its water into Loch a Ghlinne (7), the pails submerged to within an inch or so of the rim. Here they would remain, with the cool water lapping their sides, till Monday morning. It's then ye would have seen me take the hill track with a lithesome step! For there would be cream in the milk pails; cream as thick as butter; cream that could be spread on a bannock as a miner would spread toasted cheese on his 'pit piece'. Sometimes, too, I'd be taking a few handfuls of meal with me and a drop of sugar. This latter only if the Calliaich (8) wasn't looking – for sugar was scarce in these days. With the meal and sugar, and cream from the milk pail, I'd be makin' a dish (not unlike that which you term "brose") and there, on Monday morning, would be eating it with as much relish, I suppose, as ever did a mainlander the last slice of his Sunday joint. Och, aye! The summer milkin' had its joys, too! Sometimes when I will be looking back across the years, in the acquired knowledge of a decade's sojourning on the mainland, I'll just be saying to myself – "How much have I, and yet how little!"

ON CONTENTMENT

Life in St Kilda then had few of the complexities that life holds for everybody today. The thing called civilisation hadn't spoiled us. Poor we were, certainly! But we had riches, too – riches that money can't buy; for, if it could, the world today would know more about contentment than it does. After all, to be poor, and have no standards by which to measure your poverty, may on a little reflection, be just as happy a state of society as that where poverty flourishes side by side with plenty. Many a time I wonder if there is such a thing as contentment. In those days when I ate my brochan in Gleann Mor I knew more of it perhaps. Still, even there I would know something of discontent. Before the end of the season I'd be sick of the hill track. Nor would I be the only one. When autumn came, and the first tinge of brown appeared on the blaeberry leaves, when the green hills began to pale and sicken in the breath of the gall, you would see us—Morag, Kate and Rachel—och! and mony mair forby, all sitting on the hillside counting the days till the men would come with the bourocks and lead the cattle down to the village and their winter quarters. Then would ye be kennin' the meaning of the lines by which I've prefaced this article. For it would be then "Goodbye to Gleann Mor and the summer milking, to the hill track and the pail!"

Notes

[1] "Gleann Mor" – (big glen) – the most fertile part of the island.
[2] "Oiseval" and "Dun" – ("Eastfell" and "Fort") – Oiseval is the point on the right guarding the entrance to Village Bay. Dun is that on the left. Indeed, Dun is really an island: a rugged headland separated from the main island by the narrowest of channels – just as if it had been sliced off by the sword of some mighty giant.
[3] "Prettyfoot" – Cow.
[4] "Tobar Nam Buaidh" – ("Well of Virtue") – This is but one of the many religious wells for which the island is famous. It was customary when any of us were ill to go to this well for water. If

we spoke to anyone going or coming, the virtue of healing would pass from the water.

5 "Tigh na Banagaish" – ("House of the Amazon") – One of the ancient underground dwellings to which is attached many strange legends.

6 "Lochmaddy" – Port in North Uist where any surplus cattle from the island were disposed of.

7 "Loch a Ghlinne" – (Loch of the glen) – A sea loch at the back of the island, known also as North Bay.

8 "Calliaich" – Old woman.

PART VI *Hamilton Advertiser*, 11 January 1930

DR JOHNSON AND THE HEBRIDES

St Kilda first made its appearance in literature in the year 1698 by the publication of a volume which may be said to have caused something of a stir in the ranks of the literati of that period. The volume, 'A Late Voyage to St Kilda,' by M. Martin Gent., is, I gather, one of the much-sough-after prizes of the collector.[69] It is a book-man's book: one that has little literary merit, and yet one that has considerable literary interest.

This interest is not wholly centred in the fact that it is the first book to deal, in a somewhat crude and inaccurate way, with St Kilda and its people, but rather, I think, because it is regarded by all lovers of literature as the initial starting point for Doctor Johnson's tour of the Hebrides three-quarters of a century later.[70]

---

[69] Martin Martin, *A Late Voyage to St Kilda* ... (London, 1698).
[70] Samuel Johnson, *A Journey to the Western Islands of Scotland* (London, 1775), and James Boswell, *The Journal of a Tour of the*

The book, like most works of that period, was published in London. It had immediate success. It landed in the midst of a literary circle not quite so severely critical as the circle of fifty years later. Therefore, they gave the book their blessing, forgot all about its literary shortcomings in the wonder and novelty of its story. And surely there was novelty in plenty in reading, for the first time, an account of the little island some forty miles west-north-west of the Sound of Harris, where its population of two hundred lived somewhat like cavemen of old, eating the simplest yet coarsest of food, and wearing the most grotesque apparel?

FIRST IMPRESSIONS ARE LASTING

Prior to the publication of this volume little was known about the island save, perhaps, for the stories of occasional mariners—old shellbacks—whose yarns, no doubt, would be regarded as more colourful than accurate. The appearance of Martin's volume, however, instead of dismissing the "beer-shanty" stories as untrue, showed that in essence, at least, they were quite well founded. People read the book, and marvelled. It is said that the father of the future author if "Rasselas"[71] gave it to his son to read when he was but a boy attending school in his native Lichfield. It thrilled the youthful moralist; thrilled him to such good purpose that, it may be averred, on the day he read it (this first published story of my rude forefathers),[72] he went in spirit to the Hebrides. There and then he trimmed and lit that light which through intervening years was to burn steadily for his coming. The rising of "forty-five," and the darkness that fell on the isles—the aftermath of Culloden—only made the light more enchanting to Johnson. No doubt it flickered awhile in the

---

Hebrides with Samuel Johnson, LL.D. (London, 1785)
[71] Samuel Johnson, *The History of Rasselas, Prince of Abissinia* (1759).
[72] Rude forefathers is a line from 'Elegy Written in a Country Churchyard' by Thomas Gray.

breath of the fierce controversy which heralded the appearance of MacPherson with his bundle of Ossianic[73] fragments. But it didn't go out. The light only flickered to flame anew. And when, later, he made the acquaintance of his future fellow-traveller and biographer, James Boswell, it was only to see it give place to a flaming torch – a torch that, ten years later, lit the shadows on the road to the isles. Many a time I will be wishing it had lit a path to St Kilda; for, if it had, the "Journal of A Tour to the Hebrides" would have been enriched still more by many a gripping page. Save perhaps for saintly Icolmkill – Iona, no island in the west could have furnished the "sage of Baultcourt" with a finer theme to discourse upon than St Kilda.

Even then, when the weight of sixty odd years hung heavy on his step, he won no nearer to St Kilda than the castle of Dunvegan, in Skye. Here he was the guest of St Kilda's proprietor, the grandfather of the late Norman Magnus MacLeod, who, as twenty-third chieftain of the MacLeods, died a few weeks ago at Harsham, in Kent, in his ninetieth year. During his stay in the ancient castle of Dunvegan, Johnson asked many questions about St Kilda and its people. He learned from the lips of the young chief that St Kilda had been part of the MacLeod estate for generations – since that time when, following the Battle of Largs and the overthrow of Hakon, the isles of the west had passed forever from Norwegian dominance. St Kilda itself is proof that it, too, knew a language other than Gaelic, or Erse.

SOME TRADITIONAL NOTES ON ST KILDA'S OWNERSHIP

Together with the island of Harris, Uist, Skye, Raasay, and all other lands pertaining to the MacLeods, St Kilda was only acquired by

---

[73] James MacPherson, *Fragments of Ancient Poetry, Collected in the Highlands of Scotland, and Translated from the Gaelic or Erse Language* (1760) and *The Works of Ossian* (1765).

that family as the result of a marriage. Here are the traditional facts. Leod, son of the King of Man, desiring to add to the already extensive lands owned by that ancient kingdom, made a pilgrimage to Skye, where he laid siege to the heart and hand of the heiress of the MacRaits, the original owners and builders of Dunvegan's old stronghold. Leod was successful in his suit, with the result that St Kilda and all the other islands mentioned became in turn part of the ancient Kingdom of Man. The male heir of this union was therefore given the prefix "Mac," which means "son of," so that MacLeod is really son of Leod, descendant of Black Olaf, King of Man, who submitted to Alexander III. Hitherto this ancient kingdom had been for centuries but a vassal kingdom to the Kings of Norway.

DOCTOR JOHNSON'S SLY ALLUSION

I cannot be certain at this late day whether particulars so full were given by the young chief of the MacLeods to Dr Johnson on that memorable Sunday, 10th September, 1773, in the Castle of Dunvegan. But of one thing I am certain—thanks to the facile pen of Boswell—and that is, that the island of my birth was very freely discussed. Boswell informs us that when the question of Lady Grange's imprisonment in the island was being commented upon, the Doctor observed "that if the young chief would but make it known that he had such a place for naughty ladies he might make of it a profitable island."[74] The statement has, of course, more wit than wisdom. Nevertheless, it was just such a statement as likely to cause the MacLeod some embarrassment. He didn't hear it, however, for it was made in the presence of the diarist only. Had the young chieftain overhead it he might have

---

[74] Quote taken from 'Sunday, September 19' section of Boswell's *Journal of a Tour to the Hebrides*. It is not clear which edition Christina would have been using.

concluded that Johnson meant that the encarceration of Lady Grange was of some profit to his forefathers. And who will deny that maybe Johnson was right? Subsequent historians have hinted at the fact that the MacLeods of Dunvegan, together with their taxman and the minister of St Kilda, were all implicated in the plot of stopping Lady Grange's mouth. It appears that she had certain documents which were highly embarrassing not only to her husband, James Erskine of Grange, but also to his brother, John, Earl of Mar. Had the contents of such been divulged to the Government of the day, it may be safe to aver that they would have had disastrous repercussions in the MacLeods and other Scottish and Highland families, whose fortunes had already suffered as a result of the premature rising in 1715.

THE MACLEODS AS LANDLORDS

If, as the big, heavy, ponderous Doctor slyly observed then, St Kilda was of some Profit to the MacLeods, I will be all for saying now that it must have been the only occasion in their long centuries of proprietorship when it yielded any return. No doubt there were taxmen in the past who squeezed my forefathers for the last drop of oil. Historians will be telling you how they robbed them of all their cows' and ewes' milk from May Day to Michaelmas; took, by way of tenth, their every second ram-lamb and every seventh ewe-lamb; bought their feathers at approximately three shillings a stone to sell them for four times as much-and all this, and more, in the names of the great MacLeod, to whom the taxman paid the privileged sum of twenty pounds per annum. While I do know that such a practice once obtained on the island (tradition tells me so), still it never existed in my day. Nor will I be believing that Dunvegan's chiefs were aware of it. One can readily imagine a taxman of old stooping to such infamy. But Rory MacLeod? – never! If you'll be knowing aught of Hebridean lore, of its song and story, then you'll have read of Rory Mor MacLeod – big Rory, who once on a day led

Dunvegan's kilted warriors in Birlyns o'er the Minch, and o'er the Irish Sea to Ulster, where he gave his claymore in support of red Hugh O'Donnel in his fight with the English Crown. Rory, who has made Dunvegan famous in song and story, to stoop to such a practice! – again, never! But let me back to Dunvegan and Doctor Johnson.

JOHNSON AND ANOTHER ST KILDA PUBLICATION

There is still another book which exerted very considerable influence on Johnson, entitled a "History of St Kilda." by the Rev. Kenneth MacAulay. This book was also published in London in 1764, at about the time he (Johnson) made the acquaintance of Boswell, and so highly did he think of it that he made a special call upon its author during this memorable tour of the Hebrides in the autumn of 1773, which has occupied a considerable part of this paper. The learned divine was somewhat shy and diffident in the presence of the great one; so much was this in evidence that Johnson delivered himself of a judgement which nowadays no serious student of literature will attach any importance to. The Rev. Keuncth MacAulay was, like so many Scottish men of letters, a son of the Manse. He was sent to St Kilda after succeeding his father as sole pastor of Harris on a special church mission. His account of that visit of enquiry is graphically and scholarly chronicled in his book – perhaps the most intensely interesting of all the publications dealing with my island home. Two winters ago a first edition of this, and Martin's "Voyage," were kindly lent my husband and I by the late Dr Joseph Sutherland, of the county Orthopaedic Hospital, Stonehouse, whose death last spring was a blow to the county. Perhaps I ought to record in passing that his unbounded love for all that was best in the literature of the Gael was no less marked than his love for the suffering ones under his care. The love of good books and the love of little children were undoubtedly the late Dr Sutherland's "vade mecum" to happiness. His library contained many excellent volumes, all of which have,

I believe, been catalogued by his faithful friend, Dr MacKinlay of The Manse, Stonehouse.

Next Week I intend telling you of the bird of ill omen, and about the bombardment of the island by a German submarine.

PART VII *Hamilton Advertiser*, 18 January 1930

THE ILL-OMENED BIRD AND THE BOMBARDMENT OF THE ISLAND

Everybody knows, I suppose, that St Kilda is one of the greatest bird sanctuaries in the world; that it is visited annually by millions of sea birds which take up their quarters in its rocky fastnesses, lay their eggs, hatch out their young, and spend otherwise a life of industry; making periodic excursions to sea, where they fish for their own food, and that of their young.

It is wonderful to watch those fishing parties come home as twilight deepens. Each seems to know its own spot on the cliffs. As the flock of birds approach they will separate, as if at a signal, and make for the place where their young await them. On the cliffs of Ruival, Carn Mor, Connachair – indeed all round the island as steep sides are literally painted white with the forms of feathered fishers. For every cliff bird is a fisher-and a deft and clever one too! I have watched gannets, fulmars and guillemots swoop upon their prey from the dizziest of heights. Level with the cliff tops of Connachair I've seen them hover on the wing like hawks, suddenly to plunge to the ocean a thousand feet below. Should you stand here on a summer night, when the sun is dropping to its ocean bed, and the sky is roseate with those alluring tints reflected from a sunlit sea, it is to be violently reminded of two extremes – the tranquil peace and beauty of sea and sky, and the awful noise of the birds. All down the cliff face the little sea parrots will be hovering, like insects on the wing, emitting a chattering sound which, added to the screaming of whirling fulmars and gillemots, is like the sound we generally associate with a huge concourse of excited people. To describe it accurately is beyond my pen. It must be heard to be appreciated.

THE BIRD OF ILL OMEN

Of all the birds that visit the island there is but one in which who stand in dread, namely, that "mainland dweller with the two note call" – the cuckoo. It is the bird of ill omen. Seldom does it visit the island, but, when it does, it is the herald of some impending local tragedy or national calamity. Superstition? Perhaps! Still, it is strange how that, when its note is heard, something of a tragic nature is sure to follow. On reflection one knows that such is merely coincidence. And yet, how often do we all try to unravel that which is so uncannily associated with the phrase "talk about the devil and he's sure to appear!" The cuckoo is not a regular visitor. Sometimes many years elapse between its visits. When it does make a call it is much earlier in the year than we are in the habit of hearing it in the country. The bird of mystery seems just to use the island as a halting place on its way to more favourable quarters, for it tarries but a little while. If its note is heard one day it is sure to be missed the next. When a little girl, and the news of Queen Victoria's death came to the island, we all said in the same breath "I was sure that's what the bad bird meant!" It was heard early in the spring of 1908[75] when a disaster involving the lives of three natives (two of whom were my brothers) took place in the bay near the rocks of Dun. They tell me, too, that the

---

[75] It was actually 1909.

year two fowlers went to their doom over the cliffs of Connachair it had been piping out from a spot on the hills above the village. When the German submarine bombarded the island during the war the natives recalled how that a day or two previously they had trembled to its call. Yes, we don't like to hear the cuckoo, it is verily the bird of ill omen.[76]

The following account of the bombardment of St Kilda by a German submarine some three months prior to the signing of the Armistice, and given me by eye-witnesses on a later visit to the island, is perhaps well worth recounting, even at this late day, because of the very humane character of the submarine commander, and the spirit of chivalry which he then exhibited. Not unlike the commander of the raider "Emden"[77] (a vessel somewhat notorious in naval history), his conduct helps to relieve the ugly picture of war of some of its black spots. Here is the full account as given me:–

ECHO OF THE GREAT WAR

It was on the morning of May fifteenth 1918, that the islander on watch, high above the village, signalled the naval station of the approach of a submarine on a course east by south, which seemed to indicate the Village Bay as its objective. On receipt of this intelligence back came the voice of the officer over the land telephone. "What nationality is she?" "She flies no colours, sir, and has no distinguishing marks by which to identify her!" said the watch. "Her conning tower is well above the water, and her deck partly awash, sir, and she seems to be standing in to the point of Osieval making for the bay!" This information of the watch proved to be substantially correct, for in very short time after being

---

[76] Heathcote, writing in 1900, describes how the islanders believed that 'the cuckoo in Spring portends to the death of the proprietor' (i.e. the MacLeod laird). Heathcote, *St Kilda*, 81.
[77] Karl von Müller (1873–1923).

sighted she stole stealthily round the bluff of Osieval and lay to, ready to commence operations. Immediately all precautions were taken by the naval unit, to warn the inhabitants, while from the wireless station messages were broadcast to the patrols at sea, to the Admiralty, and the base. All was excitement on the island, as all was activity on the submarine. With the marshalling of the gun crew to their positions abaft the conning tower, and the swinging of the "eighteen pounder" into position, the hurry and bustle aboard the submarine suddenly came to a standstill. It appeared to the islanders as if, after hurriedly preparing, the Germans were somewhat loth to commence hostilities. They seemed waiting on something. For quite a time the U boat lay there just off the point of Osieval, with the sixteen little white-washed cottages offering a target easy and inviting – but never a shot! Occasionally the commander would be seen to sweep the village with his glass then turn and speak to his leading gunner, as if saying "No, not yet!"

At length, after what must have been an eternity to that U boat commander, the women and children were seen to take to the hillside, going up and over out of range of his projectiles.

Only then did the bombardment begin. The objective was the wireless station, and wholly upon it and a few Admiralty huts was its fire concentrated. The huts were soon reduced to matchwood, but the station, despite round after round of deliberate fire, was working again within a few moments of the close of the action. I am informed that the operators continued sending calls till a shell came in under the roof and partially buried them in a shower of debris. In all seventy shells were fired. As was to be expected one or two of the projectiles ricocheted, with the result that a dwelling on the left and the church on the right were both slightly damaged. St Kildians, while they cannot praise the marksmanship of the German gunners, will long continue to praise the consideration shown them by the commander. Many a time I will be reflecting on what might have been had another of those sea pirates got its gun trained on the island. From what I could gather from my brothers and sisters it appears that the

German commander did exactly what he came to do. What he might have done, he didn't – and naturally, as an isleswoman, I am thankful. He might easily have destroyed the people and their dwellings, leaving the village a shambles, and thereby solving the problem of St Kilda and what to do with its handful of souls.

SOME EXPLANATIONS

There is little doubt that the commander of that submarine knew more about the island than was to be expected from an enemy. Perhaps the following story may help to throw some light on the matter. I have had the truth of it vouched for, so that it is no fictitious tale. Sometime prior to the bombardment a British vessel (unarmed) was surprised by a German submarine some ten to fifteen miles north west of the island. Its crew were ordered to the boats, a charge placed aboard, and the vessel blown up. This accomplished, the commander, speaking in excellent English, asked the British crew if they knew exactly where they were, and being answered in the negative, he instructed them in the course to set for St Kilda, which he accurately described. He told them of how it but infrequently received a mail, and, in short, everything that was really worth knowing. Naturally, the British crew were surprised; but, can you judge of their amazement when, after proceeding a few boats length on their way another member of the submarine crew, speaking also in excellent English, cried out: "When you get to St Kilda see if old Neil has still a drop in the medicine bottle!" The only explanation one can offer for the Germans knowledge of the island, its people, and its medicine bottle is that in all probability the member of that crew was in pre-war days associated with one or other of the many strange trawlers which the winds of chance occasionally blew into the bay. He had received hospitality at the hands of the islanders. And he hadn't forgotten. Or, again, this German may have been a deck hand on one of the whalers that, for long years, frequently used St Kilda bay as a safe anchorage for their whales prior to removing them to the whaling station of West Loch, Tarbert, in Harris. It was on board just such a vessel that I crossed to be married. My husband-to-be accompanied me on the journey. He had won my mother's consent, so we set out in the care of a big, bronzed, and weather-beaten Norwegian – a veritable son o' the sea. Behind the rolling tub of an evil smelling whaler four monsters of the deep were in tow, their skins inflated (as is the custom) to give them buoyancy. A cloud of birds that darkened the heavens and made the day hideous with their clamouring kept swooping ever down for a pick from the scaly, vermin-laden hides. 'Ugh! I can smell the odour after seventeen years as if it came in through the window! Unless you have a constitution of iron and an appendage that is smell proof don't travel far in a whaler.

HOW AN ISLESMAN KEPT HIS WITS

A good story was told me, during my subsequent visit to the island, of an old islander who would not, at first, believe it was a German submarine. He sauntered down to where the men were taking cover and began appealing to them to launch the boat, expressing himself very eloquently with the only English he was capable of that it wasn't a German. In the period of waiting he kept pointing out to sea, saying the while, 'British! Plenty tobacco! British! plenty tobacco!' When the first crash broke the stillness, however, Old Findlay[78] collapsed flat beside the rest, cursing and praying alternately. After the bombardment ceased an argument arose as to the exact number of shells fired. The dispute was settled by the old fellow producing a piece of stick with a mark for every shot fired. He had kept his wits.

My next and concluding article, will deal with New Year Customs, etc.

---

[78] Finlay MacQueen, Christina's half brother.

PART VIII *Hamilton Advertiser*, 25 January 1930

NEW YEAR CUSTOMS AND CONCLUSIONS

> The flight of years-how many an eye
> Weeps at the thought of years gone by!
> Looks back upon the sad array–
> The restless night – the anxious day;
> Sees the lov'd form so pale, so chill.
> And mourns its broken idol-still!
> while all below, that soothes or cheers.
> Seems buried in the flight of years.

I am indebted to some anonymous bard for the above very fitting lines with which to introduce this, my eighth and last article of the series. Although you will be reading it in the early weeks of 1930, I am penning it as its predecessor is about to pass 'into that deep and boundless sea; into that wide eternity'.[79]

The first stroke of the midnight bell will herald for most of us a period of resolution and resolve, just as it will also herald for me the passing of that period of retrospection and review in which, for the last few hours, I have been very such absorbed. It is said that a Scot always makes for home on a Hogmanay, just as other English-speaking people do on the eve of Christmas.

I suppose it is well that it should be so; that one period of the year should find the much divided human family in a less cantankerous mood, and more ready to listen to the pleadings of the God of faith, and hope, and charity.

---

[79] For the full poem quoted at the start and end of this introduction, see *The Gem Book of Poesie; to Aid in the Development of the Religious and Moral Feelings and Affections* (1846), 107–8.

HOGMANAY IN ST KILDA

Hogmanay will be celebrated with little hilarity; with less plunking of corks and emptying of bottles than in any other part of the Empire. Only some thirty-seven inhabitants will hear the tolling of the bell, and it will be answered in much the same manner as others have answered the call of the Nativity – by prayer and thanksgiving. The dawn of a new year has ever been regarded by the natives as, not merely another numeral added to the milestone of life, but a heralding of that period when the sun commences its return journey: when the days begin to lengthen, and the birds return to the cliffs. In the old days it was customary to attend a church service at midnight. This practice has, of recent years, ceased. The natives now attend divine service at noon of New Year's Day. On New Year's Eve the children are the guests of the minister in the manse, and tonight I am thinking of the years when that treat was regarded as the most wonderful and pleasant of our very limited festivities. To the luxury of tea would be added that of a huge dumpling and biscuits – a treat which, you may be sure, was long looked forward to, and as long remembered. After tea, and the clearing away of the rough planks which served as seats, we would indulge in games not unlike your 'blind man's buff' and 'hide the thimble'. Following this came the most important event of the evening – the distribution of gifts. What a moment was for us then! The minister would unlock the old chest in which the presents had reposed for months. With heart beating like sledgehammers and eyes nearly starting from their sockets, we would watch the operation of unpacking the simple little pinafores, handkerchiefs, needle cases, and all the other paraphernalia, which a kindly old soul had gathered from all quarters and stored away for this memorable occasion.

SOME PERTINENT THOUGHTS ON TOYS

Many a time I will be wondering if the children of today are really happier in the possession of their marvellous toys than we were then with simple things. And as a mother with some experience, I scarcely think so. I may be wrong, of course, as a result of being cradled in an environment decidedly simple, which may have left an old-fashioned mark upon me. But then, there may be many more forby me who will be having that said about them: and I prefer to be regarded as old-fashioned, if it means finding joy in simple things. It strikes me that the toy shops of today are about as complex as life itself. Can it be that even toys reflect their period with as much fidelity as literature and music? It may be argued, with some degree of accuracy, too, that the very prolificy of toys makes the little ones of today as difficult to please as are their elders in the sphere of literature and music. In the latter field the craze for a new book – a something to tickle and amuse, is just as pronounced as the child's craze for a new and more brightly coloured toy. If a novel has a highly sensational and sexual tone, it becomes a best seller. If a song has a highly nonsensical lyric, and a tune with a decidedly perverted rhythm which seems to dance along like a cripple on stilts, it, too, commands the world's attention. What joy or pleasure such may afford is, however, of a much more fleeting and transient nature than that which comes from more simple or less complex sources. But enough of moralising!

NEW YEAR FESTIVITIES AND CUSTOMS

In the St Kilda, of my day and generation we observed the new year on two separate dates, i.e., January first and January thirteenth – this latter according to the old calendar. The former had all the character of a religious festival, while the latter was, in certain respects, not unlike that which we all now observe. The only tangible difference was that instead of making whisky and wine the vehicle for expressing our wish for a prosperous new year, we did so by breaking and exchanging bannocks. On the day preceding the celebration mothers would be busy baking. Next morning we would sally forth with an oaten bannock the full size of the girdle and fastened on our back by means of a kerchief. This we would convey to the dwelling of our neighbour. Here it would be taken, broken, and shared amongst the inmates, the while we kept expressing audibly the wish for a "good New Year." Immediately the bannock was broken and tasted, the good lady of the dwelling placed one of her own, in a similar fashion, upon our back, with instructions to convey it to our mother with her best wishes. This went on all day, from dwelling to dwelling. This thought underlying that custom – that age-old link with a distant past, was a very beautiful one. In short, it was but an expression of the hope that food, throughout the ensuing year, would never be absent from the dwellings; and that, should it ever be so, then, just as each shared the other's bannock, so also would they share each other's burden.

A KEY TO MEMORY

Tonight, as the year rapidly passes, and I am about to write 'finis' to these tales and reminiscences of island life, there is borne in upon me the fact that, after all, I have but imperfectly accomplished that which I set out to do. The difficulty I found in beginning is nothing to that which I experience in concluding. For, in review, I find that there are ever so many things which ought to have had a place in these memoirs, and which must remain over until some future occasion when, with your editor's permission, I may again occupy these columns. Someone has said (very wisely, I think) that there is no better key by which to unlock the cells of memory than the pen. From infancy onwards we are all guilty of making prisoners of life's happenings. We seem to number them all, too, in accordance with the amount of interest they held for us; the amount of joy or sorrow they gave us. But as time passes they seem to recede, growing smaller and smaller, just as pain diminishes with the passing of time. A word, however, may startle us, and start all those prisoners of memory to forge their link in the chain which reaches back to the past.

CONCLUSION

Even now I am reminded that the important question, i.e., 'What size is the island?' has never been answered, and in case this has already formed itself upon some reader's lips, let me now explain. 'Hirta' or St Kilda is roughly three miles long by two miles broad. Its island companions are in point of size and acreage as follows:– Soay, Boreray, Dun, Stac-an-Armin, Stac Lee, Stac Soay, Stac Biorach, Levenish, Stac Dona, and numerous lesser rocks or stacks, the group is supposed to be (according to many eminent glacialists and geologists) all that now remains of a chain of volcanoes that, in the pre-glacial period, stretched from Iceland via St Kilda and east through the Hebrides. The huge masses of rock which jut forth to an enormous height are considered the core of those ancient volcanoes. Other writers allude to the group as part of the lost continent of Atlantis, and, in support of their contention, refer to the finding, centuries ago, of the fossils of trees and the antlers of a reindeer deep in a peat bed in Gleann Mor. If such finds were actually made (which is quite feasible, although in this connection writers are merely chronicling island tradition), then it must have been possible, at some remote period, to cross dry shod from Hirta to Harris. No doubt such speculative theorising will be very interesting to those who feel the lure of the rocks and glaciers, and make these, and kindred sciences, their study. To me, such is interesting, too. But, naturally, my interest is chiefly centred in the fact that St Kilda is home – the place where slumber generations of my kith and kin. In the little whitewashed cottage that I see tonight so plainly under the hill, my first feeble cries were heard. Here, too, the father who sired me and the mother who bore me passed out on the last long voyage.

MY ISLAND HOME

In a little over a year, following the awful drowning tragedy of March, 1908, when I lost my eldest and youngest brothers, they carried my father into the deep shadow of Connachair.

Can you wonder how that to-night, when another year is about to add its numeral to the milestones stretching back, I should turn my thoughts to those who still keep a crusie lit for me?

Thirty-seven men, women and children – that is all! Just a handful! But tonight I won't be measuring St Kilda's population by the living. Those others, whom the hand of fate can never touch, present no problem to this or future governments. Safe from the distractions of modernism, the thunder of the Devil, and the poison gases of his associates, they but wait for the dawning of that glad new year – just as you and I, dear reader, wait for the dawn of 1930. Ah, yes, there's the kirk bell!

> The flight of years – 'twill soon be o'er.
> When the last pilgrim treads the shore,
> When darkness broods across the sun
> And mercy's gracious work is done.
> When heaven renewed and earth restor'd
> Shout at the presence of their Lord.
> Disease and death, and sin and tears.
> Shall perish with the flight of years.

Interlude *Hamilton Advertiser*, 1 March 1930[80]

ST KILDA INVALID SUCCOURED: HER LINK WITH THE COUNTY

Dr Shearer, medical adviser to the Scottish Board of Health for the Western Isles has, at the second attempt, succeeded in reaching St Kilda, in response to an urgent S.O.S., and removed for treatment to a Glasgow hospital, a young married Isleswoman, Mrs John Gilles, sister of Christina MacDonald MacQueen, whose interesting series of St Kilda articles occupied the columns of the *Hamilton Advertiser* recently.

Immediately on receipt of the news of Dr Shearer's first unsuccessful attempt to reach the island by the lighthouse vessel, Hesperus, a few weeks ago, a *Hamilton Advertiser* correspondent got into touch with Christina MacDonald MacQueen, who expressed the opinion then 'that the Hesperus would never clear the Sound of Harris'. Subsequent events proved the truth of her observation. She was of the opinion that a trawler, well acquainted with the island, would have had a greater chance of success.

AN UNEVENTFUL VOYAGE

After many anxious weeks the fishery cruiser, *Norma* (Captain Wright), with Drs Shearer and MacLean aboard, steamed quietly into East Bay last Sunday, after an uneventful voyage. The church service was interrupted by a blast from the *Norma's* siren, and hastily brought to a close. Old and young rushed pell mell to the rocky landing stage, where the visitors were welcomed, and the long overdue Christmas mail seized with eager hands. Some 16

---

[80] This article is not by Christina, but is added here as it reports on her sister's illness that would ultimately lead to evacuation.

bags of mails were landed. Immediately on his arrival, Dr Shearer had a consultation with the patient, whom he discovered to be in an expectant condition, and suffering from a nervous disorder, as a result of the extreme isolation of the island, and the lack of medical skill. Both doctors came to the conclusion that a little while on the mainland amongst her friends would restore her unsettled nerves.

THE PATIENT'S WELCOME

After a minute inspection of the Islanders and their dwellings (many of which are now derelict), the doctors, with their patient and her husband, embarked for the mainland after a four-hours' stay. Arriving in. Oban, the party entrained for Glasgow, where they were met on arrival on Monday evening by quite a little colony of St Kildians, whose strong and 'robust' appearance brought back vividly the words of the writer in Part I of the St Kilda series which dealt with island depopulation: – "Its youth has fled. Old age has settled like a vulture upon its rocky steeps. Hirta's day has passed!" One had only to look at the youthful appearance of that little group of islesmen and women to see the truth of those preceding words. No community can long exist – no nation can long exist that is forced to watch the passing of its youth. According to reliable island opinion, the problem of St Kilda and what to do with its scanty population, will gradually solve itself. In a decade at most the island will, in all probability, be entirely depopulated, unless, of course, the Government of that day decide to act on the hint of Dr Johnson and, instead of making it a home for naughty ladies, convert it into an asylum for wild and uproarious politicians, many of whom, even in our day would be none the worse of a lengthy sojourn in quiet places.

ST KILDA'S DESERTED DWELLINGS

After the patient had received a right Highland welcome from her friends, she was motored off to Stobhill Hospital where, at the moment, she is doing splendidly, and hopes soon to join her sister where the peace and quiet of Avondale will do much to hasten her complete recovery.

In an interesting chat with the sister of the patient, the writer learned that, of the 16 dwellings which comprise the village, seven are either totally or partially abandoned. No. 3 is unoccupied: No. 4 deserted and roofless; Nos. 6 and 8 have no tenant; No. 12 is partly occupied; Nos. 11 and 15 have each but one occupant. Fate is thus busy writing up a new chapter to the already gloomy one of Highland depopulation, so that in the near future the young men and maidens from St Kilda will be joining their voices to those of countless thousands of Gaels in the lines of Henry White (Fionn):

"I mourn for the Highlands, now drear and forsaken,
The land of my fathers, the gallant and brave."

THE CALL OF MODERNITY

What is taking place in St Kilda today is exactly and precisely what took place all over the Highlands with the advent of the present industrial system. From the middle of the 18th century onwards for a hundred years there was a steady and persistent trek on the part of the Highlanders to the throbbing centres of industry. The lure of the rapidly developing cities of the south fell on the glens and straths of the north and west in wisps of magic. The herdboy left his flocks and the maid her wheel. Their lot was east into the mad scramble and gamble which has characterised a century's effort in building up the now top-heavy and cumberous machine – a machine that, today, finds the load too much for its horse power. I remember having read somewhere in Boswell a remark made about depopulation by Johnson. To quote it from memory:– "This rage for trade will defeat itself. It is like gamesters engaged in a game for stakes. But when there is no stakes there is no gamesters, and this game—this rage for trade—will cease in the country where it is first brought to fruition." A remarkable Prophecy, and made in the Hebrides somewhere during his tour in the year 1773.

TOO LATE FOR THE SHARING

The unfortunate position of the St Kildian today is that he has heard the call of the industrial world a century too late.

> "Nothing left can the laggard discover,
> Not an inch but its owners there are"

—to quote the words of Schiller in his poem, "The Sharing of the Earth".[81] While one would rather see an effort made to rehabilitate the deserted villages of the Highlands and Islands, one cannot but feel that, after all, life on such an island as St Kilda can, at best, but offer little compensation for an anxious youth. Perhaps the best thing possible for the Islanders would be the inauguration of a more regular service of trawlers, the owners of which might have some slight assistance from the Government for the conveyance of the Island mails. This would tend to brighten the lives of the old people, who will never leave the island until they finally pass, as Christina MacDonald Macqueen says "unto the shadows of Connachair."

---

[81] Friedrich von Schiller, 'The Sharing of the Earth'.

PLATE 1: This commercial postcard was sent by Robert Chalmers to Miss Agnes Chalmers in Detroit, USA, and bears a St Kilda postmark. The message is dated Wednesday 19 July 1930. See Appendix 3 for more details.

PLATE 2: David Chalmers (1860–1946) and Neil Gillies (1896–1989) at Tobar nam Buadh, the Well of Virtues, Tuesday 18 July 1930. See Appendix 3 for more details.

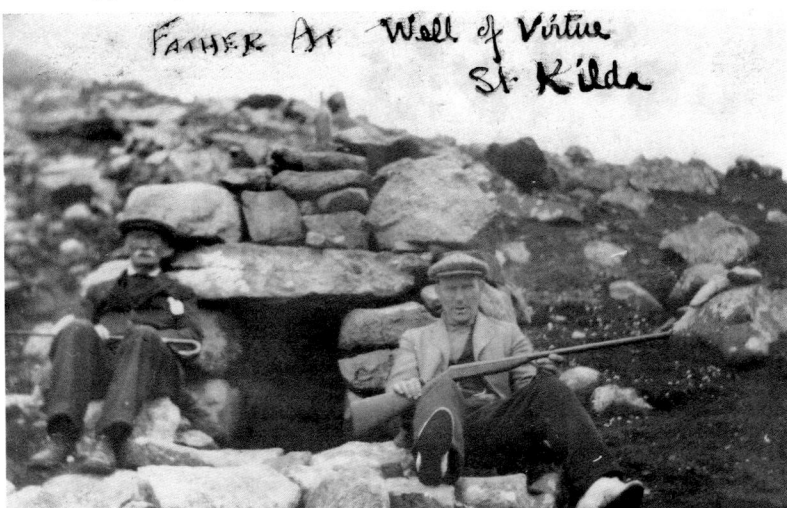

PLATE 3: Landing passengers at the quayside, at an unknown moment during Robert Chalmers' visit.

PLATE 4: A commercial postcard with a St Kilda postmark of 21 July 1930. The last man seated on the right of the picture of the bottom right is the minister Angus Fiddes, whom Christina mentions several times. See Appendix 3 for more details.

PLATE 5: One of several pictures taken by Robert Chalmers of the cliffs. This card is annotated on the back: 'THE MOST FRIGHTFUL CLIFF IN THE BRITISH ISLES "CONNACHAIR" ST KILDA. 1,350 feet. TOP SECTION. PHOTOGRAPHED JULY 31st 1930 by R. Chalmers, Lady Avenue, Stonehouse, Lanarkshire, Scotland.'

PLATE 6: A group queuing for the post office on Main Street. The man with the sheep on his shoulder is possibly Neil Ferguson Jnr.

PLATE 7: This picture also accompanied Robert Chalmers' *Hamilton Advertiser* article of 9 August 1930, with the caption 'Animated scene at St Kilda Post Office'.

PLATE 8: Left to right: brothers Ewen and Donald Gillies; the smallest boy is Norman John Gillies; Dugald Munro (the 'missionary'); Neil Ferguson Senior; probably Donald Munro (the minister's son) and possibly Donald Ewan MacKinnon (with thanks to John Gillies for identifying all these individuals).

PLATE 9: The bull was left to swim behind the rowing boat, then hoisted onto the steamer in the distance. See Appendix 3 for more details.

PLATE 10: Left to right: Finlay MacQueen, Finlay Gillies, Donald Gillies, Norman MacKinnon (with board). With thanks to John Gillies for identifying these individuals. See Appendix 3 for more details.

PLATE 11: Robert Chalmers and Christina, picture accompanying the *Sunday Post* article, 16 June 1935.

PLATE 12: 'My mother Christina MacDonald MacQueen, St Kilda, 1902'. Handwriting of Janet 'Jenny' Chalmers, her daughter. This picture (albeit mirrored) appeared alongside an article about St Kilda in the *Daily Record* of Saturday 21 August 2010: 'St Kilda the Saddest Farewell'.

PLATE 13: Christina, in her Glasgow finery, not long after leaving St Kilda. Note the contrast to her St Kilda garb in the previous photograph (Plate 12). The back of the picture has the note 'to Jenny from mother'.

My Childhood Days on Lone St Kilda

Article 1 *Dundee People's Journal*, 17 May 1930

ROMANCE AND TRAGEDY OF A SEA-GIRT ISLE

It's a little place and a lonely place, just three miles long and two miles broad, and girt by rugged and stupendous cliffs, upon which, and the season of the year, countless millions of sea birds are nesting. Mainlanders call this little island by the name St Kilda which is really a group name, I call it Hirta, which means to me just 'home'. It lies 40 odd miles West north West of the Sound of Harris – that narrow channel which forms the natural line of demarcation for a Harris man and a man of Uist.

Scattered around it, at varying distances, other islands and stacks (pyramidal rocks), some of which tower to an enormous height, giving one the impression as a distance of so many 'church steeples'. Closer inspection, however, will reveal strange and fantastic shapes in those stacks, which geologists regard as the remains of a chain of volcanoes that in the pre-glacial period stretched from Iceland through the Hebrides. Their hard, flinty, needle like points look as if they had been white washed. This is accounted for not so much by the clouds of seafowl which hover over them or nest upon them, but by the guano of the birds. They have the appearance on a summer twilight of strange wraiths risen from the deep or of ghostly ships being slowly swallowed up in the darkness. St Kilda or Hirta is, therefore, not a single island alone in the sea, as is often imagined, but simply the largest of a group of eight, all of which go to form what is perhaps one of the world's greatest bird sanctuaries.

TRAGEDY RECALLED

In the largest and only inhabited island of the group I was born upwards of 40 years ago, of parents both of whom knew little of the mainland's ways, and who I'm sure, cared less. Their speech was that of the Gael, their philosophy that of the Isles. A life of solitude, with periodic visitations of extreme hardship, had at an early stage whitened their heads with the snows of three score years, and given to their natures a calm and quiet resignation, a faith and a hope that, away beyond life's battleground, lay a place of rest and peace.

Following a severe domestic tragedy my father died, completely broken by the weight of his affliction. At midday of the 23rd of March 1908,[82] my brothers, Norman, the elder, and Ian, the younger, went to Dun, an island in the vicinity, to attend the sheep. They never returned. The boat, a Norwegian scow, which had been gifted to the natives by the skipper of a whaler, and by which they and three other companions crossed to Dun, was found floating keel up with two of the five occupants hanging onto its sides. My brothers were roped together as is the custom, and it is said that, when leaping from the boat to the landing ledge, the boat swung out, causing them to misjudge the distance, and precipitating the entire crew into the water.[83]

---

[82] It was 1909 – see Introduction.

[83] Alice MacLachlan's diary records the event 'the suspense at home was awful; the women were all down and anguished weeping and wailing, I cannot describe'. She also records the sorrow over the following days, compounded by there being no bodies washed up bar Norman or John. Quine, *St Kilda Portraits,* 105. Donald John Gillies recounts a version of this story. The aim was to see how the lambs on the island were getting on, and whether they would have enough grass to last them. Norman MacQueen was married and living at 11 Main Street, while 'John' (anglicised from Iain) was still living at home in number 10. The boat was owned by John MacDonald of 3 Main Street, and was apparently of a design unfamiliar to the

NEVER SMILED AGAIN

From that day all was dark to my father. He never again smiled as was his wont. Within a year he was carried to the rear of that little dwelling in which I was born—in which his and his sire's first feeble cries were heard—and laid to rest in the little cemetery, the encircling wall of which almost touches that of our cottage.

As I write these memoirs I am all too conscious of the present plight of the living. But the dead have a tender place in my heart, and I may tarry a little to describe this quaint little gods acre, with its tombstones made of flat slabs of rock carried from the adjacent hillsides; which have no ornamentation and none of the chisel marks of moderns, and which, to the casual observer, have no distinguishing lines, yet speak with as much eloquence and sincerity as the most magnificent marble.

In St Kilda, as in other lonely quarters of the Hebrides, the memory of the departed is perpetrated not by a show of fine sculpture, but by the more lasting monument of fine words, words with feeling and a gentle rhythm; words which, spoken or sung in the glow of the peat fire, or during the more exacting duties of the hillside or the cliffs, were the medium by which we kept alive the good deeds of our friends.

BRITAIN'S HIGHEST CLIFF

The little white washed felt roofed cottage in which I was born and in which I learned at an early age the art of spinning and plucking the birds is the tenth of the sixteen which formed the village, and which like Crescent shaped at the base of the island's highest hill, called 'Connachair' – a hill which is really only half a hill, since you cannot go up the one side and down the other.

---

islanders. The third man drowned was Donald MacDonald, while Neil MacKinnon and John Gillies survived. Gillies, *The Truth About St Kilda*, 48–9, 51, 105.

It rises steeply up from the village to well over 1000 feet, then ends abruptly, just as if some giant had split it with a sword, the back half falling out to lose itself in the sea. Connachair is therefore not only the island's highest hill but the island's highest cliff. Indeed, it is the highest cliff in the British Isles, being one thousand three hundred feet.

It is not easy to imagine what it must feel like to dangle on a rope's end over such a precipice this is what our menfolk must do to catch the fulmar – the bird that means food, the bird without which life in St Kilda would be well-nigh impossible, the bird that down through the ages has brought the island is succour, and we at times, too, sorrow. How often have we missed our men, only to find the rope frayed and parted, and then forever gone! To look down on one of the small boats going round the base of the cliff to fish is to imagine, as you see the oars rise and fall, some large bird flapping its wings. It is truly an awe inspiring sight.

In the second year of the Great War, two islesmen, John MacDonald and Ewen Gillies, went to their doom over these cliffs. You can realise what a shock it must have been to their womenfolk, who, going up with their men's tea, found, instead of the heap of birds they had expected, the loose, dangling rope, which all too plainly told its tale of tragedy. It was an autumn night towards dusk. Calling their names, but at first suspecting nothing, the women laid down their pitchers and took out their knitting to while away the moments while they waited for their loved ones appearance.

A NIGHT OF SUSPENSE

They were long in answering their signals, so they crept over to the edge of the cliff and peered down its steep face. But there was no sign of their men. Next they felt for the standing rope to which both should have been attached, but it was loose. For a second they looked at each other in silence, then fled screaming down the hill. The men of the village hurried to the scene, but darkness made it impossible to do anything.[84]

All night long women sobbed in the dwellings of Hirta, hiding their faces in their shawls and praying for the dawn. Scarcely had it flushed the east when the men were on the clifftops. The use of a telescope soon picked out the form of a body lying on a rock far down towards the water. My brother Donald[85] volunteered to go down, so they lowered him yard by yard, fathom by fathom, till eventually he reached the body, which he soon saw was beyond all human aid.

It was immediately hoisted to the top and carried reverently to the village, where it was buried in the same way and in the same place as was that of his sire before him.

The other body was never recovered. The sea round St Kilda seldom, if ever, gives up its dead. It just seems to suck them to its treacherous bosom, pulling them down, down to the horrible caverns under the cliffs.

CANNOT SWIM

Perhaps many of our drowning tragedies could have been averted if the menfolk had only learnt the art of swimming. But no St Kildian has ever yet mastered that art. My own brothers might have been alive today, and the lad who slipped with his bag of mallets[86]—fish he had caught with a rod, which resemble perch—might have been one of the party of young men now upon the mainland if he and they had not utterly disregarded the first

---

[84] John MacDonald had only been married a few weeks before, to Christina's like named niece (daughter of her elder half-brother Finlay MacQueen), Christine MacQueen – she apparently died of a broken heart soon afterwards. Gillies, *The Truth About St Kilda*, 31, 41–3.

[85] Given Christina had left the island by this point, Donald presumably informed her of this incident. The body found was that of Ewen Gillies.

[86] Presumably 'mullets'.

and most essential or requirement of those who lives are passed by the sea.

The reason for our dread of the water is because of sharks. In summer the bay is literally alive with them at times. This, however, did not deter the Reverend James Barr, M.P.,[87] many years ago, when on a visit to the island, from disporting himself in the water of the bay, to the apprehension of the natives and the apparent disregard of sharks, or even whales. Perhaps those finny marauders of the deep had some regard for the future of the church, and so spared the life of this great champion of religious freedom. It's maybe, too, that his portly frame completely scared them. In any case the reverend gentlemen can claim to have done what few would have cared to attempt.

Article 2 *Dundee People's Journal,* 24 May 1930

HOW TOURISTS SPOILED THE ISLANDERS

All sorts of names have lately been bestowed on my island home. It has been termed 'misery island', the 'island of discontent', and goodness knows how many more, all of which today to me singularly fitting and appropriate upwards of 30 years ago, when I carded and spun (in the families where there were no daughters) for the magnificent salary of 'a yard of bright coloured calico to make myself a neckerchief'. I was happy. I used to long for the

---

[87] James Barr, 1862–1949, minister and liberal (and later labour) politician.

coming of the old SS *Hebridean*.[88] In these days we didn't know precisely the date of its departure from Glasgow. But we knew it was sometime in May, so for days before its arrival I would be up on the slopes of 'Connachair' with the rest of the juvenile population watching the horizon for a sign of its smoke, and whenever it was observed away we would go careering down the hillside, shouting at the top of our voices, 'it's coming!' 'it's coming!'

They say anticipation heightens joy. I believe so, for I seriously question if ever at any period of my succeeding life I was just so happy. A yard of cloth gave me more satisfaction then than a yard of silken hose gives me now. I regarded the former as a token of appreciation for my service: the latter as 'a matter of course'.

HAPPY COMMUNITY

St Kilda in those days was a happy, carefree, independent, and unselfish community. But its independence was soon to pass. As year succeeded year, as more and more tourists began to flock to the island, there crept in amongst us a feeling of unrest. To see what lay beyond the distant peaks of Harris was my earliest ambition. I was inquisitive. I was no less so than the tourists – those early tourists who entered my mother's dwelling as if they had a right to, who peered under the very bed, who sniffed in every corner, and then asked me, with a proffer of a sassenach coin, to direct them to 'Tobar nam-Buaidh', The well of virtue.[89]

---

[88] George Murray, schoolmaster of St Kilda 1886–87 describes the arrival of the *Hebridean* on 2 September 1887, and how the tourists bought stockings and tweed from the islanders. Kerr, *George Murray*, 54–5.

[89] Norman Heathcote, writing in 1900, described how 'the tourists treat them as if they were wild animals at the zoo. They throw sweets to them, openly mock them, and I have seen them at the church door during service, laughing and talking, and staring in as if at an entertainment got up for their amusement'. Heathcote, *St Kilda*, 69–70.

Those early tourists spoiled us. They weakened our faith in ourselves. They made us regard their annual visitations and their gifts in precisely the same fashion as I now regard my silk hose. In short, they became indispensable. Succeeding years saw our indifference diminish, our boldness increase. Now we boarded their vessel to sell, then they entered our dwellings to buy. Looking back across the years there comes to me the picture of the old tourist vessels with their kindly though inquisitive passengers. Everyone generally bought a box of sweets which we consumed so eagerly that had the vessel returned on the following day its tourists would have found us with our faces enveloped in a sock of salt.

INDISPENSABLE

Salt was the indispensable elements in our lives. Almost everything we ate was salted. The August catch of fulmars were put into casks after having been plucked, split, and cleaned. Our mutton was salted, because we killed our sheep when fat, during the fall, and were thereby saved the necessity of killing the emaciated creatures during the winter. The winter itself was generally accompanied by terrible storms of wind and rain and snow – the latter of which didn't lie long, owing to the salt – the salt of the sea. The storms of winter killed more sheep generally than we were able to consume. Indeed, whole flocks have been destroyed, being blown from their shelters over the cliffs and into the sea, which raged and fumed with such intensity that its prey was continually drenching the island.

During the long nights we carded and spun – that is, the women did so. The men wove; weaving upon looms as antiquated as the old turf home of 'Lady Grange', which lies before our door.[90]

This old 'cleet' (house for storing peat) was the prison home for eight weary years of the wife (only in name) of John Erskine

---

[90] Lady Grange is Rachel Chiesley, Lady Grange (1679–1745), wife of James Erskine, Lord Grange (1679–1754) whose brother was John Erskine, Earl of Mar (1675–1732). Christina mistakes 'James' for 'John'.

of Grange – a brother of John, Earl of Mar, known to students of Jacobite history as the 'bobbing John' of the '15 rebellion.

LADY GRANGE

Lady Grange's dwelling and my early years were so interwoven that I cannot refrain from telling something about the lady of sorrow, she who (according to island tradition) used to go to the rocks in spring and pray. As the first sheerwater came with its hint of summer, she went to the rocks, and, kneeling in supplication, invoked the aid of God for her deliverance. In 1742 she was rescued by her friends, after a quarrel with the proprietors' tacksman and the island missionary, and hastened to Tiumphan in Skye, where she was buried, as befitted one so marred by tragedy, in the little churchyard adjoining the church where, two centuries earlier, the MacLeods of Waternish were massacred by the MacDonald's of North Uist. Lady Grange, though not of our race and speech, must have been well beloved by my ancestors, for her name has been handed down with reverence from father to son from generation to generation.

This lady was seized by a party of ruffians in the pay of her rascally husband while in residence at Polkemmet in Stirlingshire, and, bound upon a highland pony, was led to the coast, where she was shipped, first to Heskit [Heisgeir] in the Outer Hebrides, then finally to St Kilda. Implicated in her abduction was not only James Erskine, her husband, but, as historians hint, the MacLeods of Dunvagen, then, as now, the proprietors of the island. Those who know Jacobite history – that subtle, intriguing history of the first 50 years of the 18th century – will be able to assign a reason for the spiriting away of this Lady of Sorrow.

ISLAND CUSTOMS

Much nonsense has been written of late about the remaining remnants of my race. St Kilda today is no more an island of beggars than we are today a nation of paupers. It is only true to say that they have been swept into the same quagmire of economic falsity as the whole world is floundering in. We feed a million in idleness. Can we not feed the last handful of old people who will soon pass to the shadows? Surely!

But our island customs. We were very devout in my young days, attending church at least three times a week. During communion we went on Thursday, Friday, Saturday, twice on Sunday, and rounded it off with a fore noon service on Monday. We loved the church. I still love its message, which, amid all life's complexities, is the one sure and certain solace. I remember an occasion when an old woman, far gone in sickness, had to be left alone while the others attended the church, but scarcely had they gone when she rose and, with nothing on but a gown, made her way to the service and sat on the doorstep. When we found her there we've remonstrated with her, but her only reply was, 'I had just to hear God's word'.

We had no love of dress. What we wore as a costume was made by our menfolk – just a one piece dress of coarse blue serge, invariably no boots or shoes, and with a bright coloured neckerchief of small tartan shawl fastened over our head like a gypsy. To distinguish the married women from the single, a white frieze was worn by our mothers under the shawl. That was the fashion in my day, for everyday of the week, Sunday included. In summer my work was to store peats in the little conical huts on the hillsides, to attend the cattle in Gleann Mor (big glen), to help at the waulkin' of the tweed, knit gloves and stockings for sale to visitors, and other varied duties connected with the home and the croft.

READY FOR WINTER

Autumn generally found us with plenty to do. It was the season of real and earnest preparation for the winter to follow. The men went to the fowling on the same day as mainland sportsmen go to the grouse, i.e., August 12th.

A day or two previous, every rope in the village had to be tested. This was done by fastening one end to a large boulder, then having it pulled by four men. If it resisted their efforts to break it was regarded as safe. And it had to be, for the men carried their lives on those ropes. Over precipices 1000 feet high they were lowered to the ledges, where, roped together in pairs, they carried out their harvesting.

We carried up to them their food. At the end of the day we carried home their catch to the sharing place, where they were parted. During this function each representative of the sixteen homes would be grouped around the heap waiting for his portion.

What mattered it if one couple killed 50 and the other couple only 5. Each got according to his need. It could not have been otherwise. We leaned upon each other. We had to. To appreciate the full application of the maxim, 'each for all and all for each' you had to see the men on the cliffs where a wrong move or false step meant sure and certain death.

After the sharing of the birds they had to be plucked and cleaned, seeing that the oil was extracted from their gullets and saved in jars and in little bladders. The bladders hung there till needed, with the rest for our 'cruisies' – a little saucer-like implement of metal bent up on the side having a spout from which a wick burned and a handle with an eye which fastened to a nail in the roof beam. The residue of the oil was bartered with the tacksman for provisions, as was the soft down and feathers of the birds. After plucking and cleaning they were salted into barrels as our winter food. If we had a stormy August we were hungry in spring. For we could not get to the cliffs between the 12th and 20th of the month as the young birds were all on the wing. Then it was calamity indeed.

Article 3 *Dundee People's Journal*, 31 May 1930

BLACK PERIOD IN THE ISLAND'S HISTORY

The day on which the S.S. *Hebrides* will leave Glasgow for St Kilda this summer on its usual visit will mark the second centenary of the most tragic voyage ever made to the island. To me, as to all St Kildians on the mainland, the occasion is not without significance, for it recalls the only period in history, when the population of the island was lower than it is today, and when its need for sympathy or succour was infinitely greater.

When the Hebrides, with its tourists and its stores, drops anchor in Parsons Bay it will find that the population is just some 60 per cent less than when it first commenced to visit the island some 30 years ago. It will find exactly what it expects to find – unless something unforeseen happens in the interval. But 200 years ago the first, and only, boat of the year to visit my island home found not the 180 inhabitants as it had expected, but a little broken-hearted group of 18 children and one grown male (history gives the latter number as four, tradition as one). Perhaps the story will be of some interest – it was the one story at the recounting of which I used to sit and shudder. And further, it explains the reason for the natives' age-old dread of infection, and for the prevalence of those annual epidemics of influenza which always seemed to assail us after a visit from strangers.

AFTER A YEAR

It was on a morning in May, 1730,[91] when the taxman's vessel, then en route for the island, had its attention arrested by the frantic signals of what appeared to be a party of men on the rock of Stac-an-Armin – an island some six miles off St Kilda. On approaching they were discovered to be natives of the island, but so emaciated and marked by want and exposure as to be almost unrecognisable. They were dressed in fowl skins. Their beards, long, uncut, reached to their middle; and their hair, matted and unkept, hung low upon their shoulders, giving them the appearance, as they knelt on the ledge thanking Providence for their deliverance, of beasts instead of humans.

To their rescuers they told how, a year earlier, they had been landed on the rock expecting to be called for in the course of a few days, as was the custom by the island boat. But it never returned.

At first it was thought that the boat had been wrecked in beaching, and that willing hands would soon repair it, but as the days and weeks and months rolled by, all sorts of thoughts came to torture those marooned fowlers. They knew that something of a very serious nature had occurred. What was it?

As they made towards Parsons Bay in the taxman's Birlyn, their eyes sought the rocks where, beneath the site of the present church they fondly expected to see the whole population await their arrival, shouting and making signals of welcome. The population was there, but it was all juveniles.

Tradition has told of how they wept and tore their hair and wished that death had claimed them on the rock of Stac-an-Armin. During their absence death, in the form of a plague of smallpox, had swept the island. It had been brought by a party of natives from Harris, where one of their number died and, ignorant of the

---

[91] It was actually 1728, the epidemic starting the previous year. See introduction. Christina also got the years wrong in her article for the *Hamilton Advertiser* of 14 December 1929.

nature of his death, his comrades had brought home his belongings. This happened immediately following the departure of six fowlers to Stac-an-Armin, and accounted for the non return of the island's only boat. Its crew had perished.

When the present dwellings were being built in 1868 the bones of those who succumbed in that most gruesome of island tragedies were uncovered. They (the victims) had been hastily and unceremoniously buried in graves immediately in front of each cottage door, and tradition tells of one survivor, who carried out the gloomy task of digging those graves, and in which occupation he was engaged from dawn until dark.[92]

DREAD OF DISEASE

The mere writing of this is suggestive of the presence of spirits; spirits of those who in the old days were in the flesh, and who used to sit at their spinning wheels and converse in whispers of that sad period in the life of their forefathers – for the blood of those folk of the past flows in the veins of the present generation through centuries of intermarriage.

The years immediately following the plague of 1729–30 saw the island repeopled by crofters from Harris and Skye. Their offspring mingled their blood with the children of the plague period, and so there came right down through the centuries that feeling of dread for all forms of infectious disease. Today, with all its apparent hardship and privation – although, mark you,

---

[92] Christina has been mistaken slightly here. The crescent of Village Bay was laid out in 1834, some hundred years after the epidemic. Prior to this the St Kildans' dwellings were grouped into a tight weather-resistant cluster. Rebuilding the modern cottages began in 1861. That said, there is no reason that during the 1868 rebuilding that remains of the older houses and the bones were not found. Christina's house in front of the burial ground is likely to have been a place of much older settlement. Stell and Harman, *Buildings of St Kilda* (RCAHMS, 1988); Fleming, *St Kilda and the Wider World,* chapter 7.

this latter is not what is represented to be and far short of what may be noted by any shrewd observer in countless homes in the cities – St Kilda has a very clean bill of health. So far as infectious diseases are concerned, the islands at no time has been afflicted. Save the influenza, it has been perfectly free of the very ordinary epidemics which mainlanders are so well accustomed to. Measles, whooping-cough, and fever are troubles unknown. I was married, with two children, before measles assailed me, and I can say, with all St Kilda's young men and women, that I had to come to the mainland before taking the disease.

I have often been asked by people interested, 'Why is it that the spring always brings an epidemic of St Kilda news? Why is it that the inhabitants are always in dire straights then?' The answer to the first is simply that, in no place I can imagine, does winter sit so heavily, or seem too long, as in St Kilda. For the greater period of the season vessels cannot approach it unless at grave risks, so that spring invariably finds some vessel within hail, and its crew ready to listen to their pleading for a mail to be sent to them.

NOT STARVING

So far as being in dire straights and starving, nothing could be farther from the truth. Who is likely to starve [while there are][93] flocks of sheep on the hillsides? They will be short of tea and sugar, perhaps, or they may be short of birds owing to the August storms preventing them from getting to the cliffs, but starvation, actual or potential, is further from the native of my island home than it is from thousands on the mainland. In my young day it

---

[93] The article has 'and' here, although this is presumably a misprint. Incidentally, Donald John Gillies was of the contrary opinion, that starvation in the final years was a problem. The difference can probably be put down to the fact that Christina left before the major depopulation of the island, and the growing inability for the labour force of the island to meet its needs. Gillies, *The Truth About St Kilda*, 84–5.

was a cup of tea on a Sunday after coming from church. Today the young woman's life, while still hard, is luxury compared with what it was upwards of thirty years ago, when we had to perform all manner of tasks, from carrying the bags of meal and flour from the shore to the cottages to walking a hundred yards over a boulder strewn track carrying large pots of boiling oil to the factor's house.

No wonder the old minister (old Angus Fiddes[94]) put a stop to the practice. If we had tripped we would have been scalded to death. This oil was the savings for the whole year. It was kept in barrels in the byre. As it lay throughout the winter it hardened, and had therefore to be melted down again when the taxman came to measure our output. Standing with a piece of stick in hand, the island bailiff would mark thereon, with a nick, each gallon of oil you emptied into the factor's drums.

The minister made the taxman bring his oil vessels to the door of every dwelling and to save us the long and dangerous walk.

OLD CUSTOMS

The St Kildian today is but a very little removed from his brother on the mainland. He is just as fond of cigarettes and tobacco, although it seems but yesterday since I saw the old men chew the clay of their pipes for a taste of 'thick black'. I remember quite vividly when apples first came to the island, brought by Captain Walker of Aberdeen. When the top was knocked off the barrel it seemed as if someone had sent us a present of painted toys and balls or something of that sort. I remember, too, when hams were given us by a passing ship, and, not knowing what they were, we were in the act of committing them to the sea when old Angus Fiddes happened on the scene. He took charge of them, and invited all of us to the manse to taste this delicacy. That night he fried ham for the entire community. The smell came up the

---

[94] Fiddes was missionary arrived in 1889 and left in 1901.

village on the wind, and we went down the village at the double. But that's a good many years ago. At that time there was but one frying pan on the island, and the minister had it. The result was we had all to borrow it, for Angus shared out the hams.

I have met many notables in St Kilda, from writers on geological and botanical subjects to Cabinet Ministers – this latter in variance to the statement which recently appeared in the press that Mr MacDonald, the Liberal Member of Parliament for the Isles, is the first M.P. to visit St Kilda. I might say that another statement about the existence of a colony of St Kildians in London is pure imagination. There are no St Kildians in London. There never have been – except, perhaps, when Mr Ferguson the well-known Glasgow tweed merchant pays it a visit on business. Mr Ferguson will be going out to the island soon. He will see great changes, and he will feel the force of them. For I think it would be difficult to find one who has more love and done so much for the St Kildians of his generation. He has been untiring in his efforts to assist every young man and woman who has left the island during the last few years. His father was bailiff of the island, as his brother is today – an old isleman of sterling worth, a careful and conscientious administrator, and an excellent Gaelic preacher. Many and many a time he took the service in the absence of a minister, and it is amongst my happiest recollections to have heard him preach.

SPIRIT OF RESTLESSNESS

St Kilda has given a few sons to the Church, the most notable perhaps being the Rev. Donald Ferguson, of Ayr. They must all feel both shocked and amused at much that is said about St Kilda. All that is wrong with the island today is just what is wrong with humanity. It has discovered that thing in life which produces restlessness. I cannot blame its young men and women. I felt restless myself, and 30 years ago I did what they are now doing – I got out. At 17 years of age I had not seen a horse, a train, or even a tree. Perhaps it will seem even more obvious how ignorant I was when I tell you I didn't even know what an ordinary 'bumble bee' was. Honey and the insects which make it were, and are, entirely unknown to the island. There is practically no flora. Only 'dockens' and nettles and sea vegetation.

I left home because I wanted to. I was the first woman to do so following the clearance of 1855,[95] when a party of islands, amongst whom were my father's uncles, left the island for Australia. The party numbered 30, many of whom died.[96] My father's uncles, with their families, started sheep farming in the outskirts of Melbourne, Victoria, and in the course of time the spreading city enveloped their place: hence the fact that Melbourne's most fashionable suburb is today called St Kilda.[97] Many letters insufficiently addressed go there and others intended for Australia have come to us.

Can you imagine my feelings, when, in the warm glow of the peat fire, I'd sit listening to my father recount the passing from the island of this friends – the MacQueens of 1855? Can you imagine my feelings when, on the eve of going to the altar, I was waiting upon by a young clergyman whose features resembled those of my own brother, and who, when he first beheld me, said, 'Why, you are just like Christina!'

'But I am Christina,' I answered.

---

[95] It was actually 1852. Christina elsewhere gets the dates of the 1727/8 epidemic confused as 1729/30.

[96] The number was 36 in total. The MacQueens that left Hirta in 1852 were Finlay MacQueen and his wife Christina, with their children Malcolm, Rachel (died en route) and John; and a second Finlay MacQueen and his wife Catherine (both dying on the voyage) and their children, Donald, Ann, Marion, Catherine, Neil, Finlay and Mary (the latter two dying on the way). Harman, *An Isle Called Hirte*, 133.

[97] The area of Melbourne was actually named after a yacht, *The Lady of St Kilda*, which was owned by Sir Thomas Dyke Acland, who often visited Hirta, not be emigrants. Hutchinson, *St Kilda*, 125–6.

'Yes,' he replied. 'But the Christina I'm thinking of is my sister in Australia.'

He, Rev. Malcolm MacQueen, was a grandson of the first of those early colonists who returned to see the island of his forefathers. The news of my impending marriage had reached him in Edinburgh, so he came, just to be there to assist, and to pray for one whose sire and his were from the same island stock.[98]

Interlude *Hamilton Advertiser*, 31 May 1930

This article is not by Christina

ST KILDA'S POPULATION STILL FURTHER REDUCED
NATIVE'S TRAGIC DEATH IN GLASGOW HOSPITAL
DECEASED WOMAN'S COUNTY CONNECTION

The St Kilda lady whose tragic death in a Glasgow hospital was announced by the press early in the week, and a notice of which appears in our issue today, is the younger sister of Christina MacDonald MacQueen, whose memoirs of island life were a feature of the Advertiser during the months of December and January last.

---

[98] This is possibly the Reverend MacQueen who visited St Kilda in 1900, and encouraged, without any success, islanders to emigrate to Australia. Gillies, *The Truth About St Kilda*, 17–18. A Reverend Finlay MacQueen tried the same in 1928. Steel, *Life and Death of St Kilda*, 194.

An account of her dramatic rescue from the island on February 15th in response to an SOS for medical aid, and her subsequent removal to a city hospital, was fully dealt with by a correspondent in our issue of the following week. The death of the woman, after three months languishing in a Glasgow hospital; has many tragic features. Until a fortnight ago she was anxiously looking forward to spending a time with her sister, in the peace and quiet of the country. A serious operation however, followed by the scourge of pneumonia, was more than the weakened frame could stand, and she soon began to sink. On Saturday last she spoke to her sister of the sailing on Monday of the S.S. *Hebrides*, and of her little boy, aged five, who with the other natives would be anxiously awaiting its arrival. Alas! as the first vessel of the tourist season slipped its moorings at Glasgow, the poor woman breathed her last.

THE FUNERAL

The arrangements for her interment were carried out by Mr Robert Chalmers of Stonehouse, this taking place on Wednesday at the Western Necropolis, Glasgow. The chief mourner was her husband, who accompanied her through raging seas on her tragic voyage, and who was never absent from her bedside during the long days of trial. It was a beautiful and simple service, the officiating clergyman being her brother-in-law, the Rev. Donald Ferguson, Free Church minister of Ayr.[99] All the mourners were natives of the lone isle, save one. It was a sad group indeed, that listened to the St Kilda clergyman, his voice quivering with emotion, speak lovingly of his departed sister. Almost unable to overcome his emotion, he spoke of the fathers and mothers of the young men grouped around who, while they committed their loved one

---

[99] Ann, Christina and Mary's older sister, was married to Neil Ferguson, Donald's brother. He was also John Gillie's uncle, as John's mother (Annie) was Rev. Donald Ferguson's sister.

to the grave, were unaware of her death. His words caused tears to well when he said: "She had hoped to go home to her loved ones by the vessel that is now on the last lap of the journey—it has left the sound of Harris. It is on the last forty miles, Borrera lies ahead. But our sister has gone home on the full tide. We lay her down in the cold earth, that part of her which earth claims, the rest is with her Father!"

THEIR FIRST MAINLAND FUNERAL

The service was almost exclusively rendered in Gaelic, and was the first occasion on which most of the youthful mourners had attended a funeral on the mainland. Every year sees the colony of St Kildians on the Mainland grow in numbers. Every year witnesses a steady decline in the island's population, and, at the moment, the nation waits for the answer of the Government to the natives' recent petition for complete removal to other shores. This summer will prove whether St Kilda is, or is not to be evacuated after perhaps eighteen centuries of occupation.

Article 4 *Dundee People's Journal*, 7 June 1930

WHY THE NATIVES WILL SAY 'FAREWELL'

I suppose it will only be those who, like myself, can translate 'St Kilda' into the magic word 'home' who will experience any feeling of regret that its community of souls is threatened with extinction; but the island may ere long become merely a sanctuary for sea birds.

It would be futile on my part to expect otherwise. However much I may lovingly regard it as a place of my birth—as the last resting place of my sires—I am deeply conscious that the average mainlander simply regards it as a home only suitable for the fulmar, guillemot, kittywake, puffin, and the numerous other species of sea fowl that infest it. No, I cannot imagine the 'man in the street' remaining other than passive when the last of the MacDonalds and the MacQueens, the Gillieses, Fergusons, and the MacKinnons wave their farewells to the rock that for centuries gave shelter and succour to their forefathers.

The abandonment of the island, even before the pressure of modern necessity suggested it to the inhabitants, has been urged on many grounds, one of them being the claims of economy. It has been pointed out that St Kilda makes calls upon the exchequer that are not compensated for by any income from the island.

But that was always a weak line of argument. The abandonment of St Kilda would probably mean the saving of £500 per annum; a sum equivalent to the salary of a very ordinary official of one of our national or municipal bureaucracies. And, after all, the money expended annually in bringing a modicum of comfort to the aged remnants of St Kilda's ancient race is no more than the government doles out every 10 minutes over the day to the so called 'dole'.

NO LOCAL TAXES

As a daughter of the island, however, I must take exception to the statement that the natives pay no taxes, and therefore have no right to expect assistance from the exchequer. Such is not the case – at least, not all the case. Granted, they pay no local taxes. Why should they?

As a community whose interests are self-centred and similar, they have never required the services of a policeman. They have no 'roads and bridges' problem. The same road as probably served the monks of old still serves the natives. Untaxed water flows out of the rocks in a dozen luscious springs, pure, sweet, and cool – I may add, probably the sweetest and coolest water in the world. Mr M. Martin and Mr Kenneth MacAulay, who have both written extensively on the religious wells of the island, speak of them in terms of wonder and amazement.[100]

So far as local taxation is concerned, they are the only community who have escaped the sweeping net of the post war tax gatherer. But they do pay taxes, dressed as I do every time I square the grocer's bill – taxes on tea, sugar, tobacco, and the various other commodities which of recent years have come to be regarded as indispensable.

The £500 per annum which it takes to administer the affairs of the island is no more than the natives have a moral right to expect. And further, saving that a little of it goes in old age pensions, the bulk of the sum is absorbed by the salary of the resident nurse and dominie-divine, both of whom, by the exacting nature of their duties, are worthy a great deal more financial recognition than they get.

A NATURAL CLIMAX

The proposal to remove the whole population of the island is only the natural climax to a process that has been going on steadily since I left St Kilda. The young men and women of the island are just like the young men and women of the glens – they get out as soon as they find themselves a burden on the community. That, of course, explains why there are no unemployed in St Kilda. It is too late to think of finding means to keep the younger generation on the island – though something might have been done in the nature, say, of quarrying and facing paving sets from its great natural resource is of granite and Syenite. But to me, at least, the complete abandonment of the island has always seemed inevitable.

---

[100] See footnotes X and Y.

The older men will not find it easy to settle in other surroundings, even in Harris, Uist, or any other island. They are all crofters there, and a crofter's existence is much the same anywhere. But St Kildians are more than crofters; they are fowlers – expert cragsmen, whose sires for generations have regarded the cliffs as a more productive source of food than even the soil, and since the cliffs provide them with a large proportion of their foodstuffs, it will be a big change for them if they have to win from the soil alone that which even expert agriculturists today are finding difficult to extract.

NEARER CIVILISATION

It may be said, 'but they will be nearer civilization!' I agree. But this will only add to their difficulties. They will, in all probability, speedily find that the nearer one gets to the thing called civilization, the greater are one's material requirements. In any case, to the old Islanders 'being nearer civilization' will only mean 'being further from home.'

I have seen the departure of the younger folk that has created in the older ones the desire to leave the island. What they desire in the present gloaming of their lives is that, during the winter months, they might have more frequent news from their loved ones whom fate has whirled apart like leaves in the autumn gale.

OTHER MOTIVES

That there are other motives for the wish to leave home I know well. One, at least, of its sixteen little white washed 'but and bens' is roofless, others are boarded up against the storms. The community is like a house divided against itself. Its youth has fled, refusing to be longer shackled to its primitive environment. Old age has settled like a vulture upon its rocky steeps. St Kilda's day has passed. Never since that remote period when, tradition asserts, the monks of Iona discovered it to make of it a refuge and a home; never since that equally remote period when the ancient Celtic rover and pirate, Macquin, made its caves and rocky fastness a hiding place for his booty, has the doom of its inhabitants seem so imminent.

Through the centuries, unbroken, its long line of hardy cliff men have battled with death and wrestled with privation, till now, alas, it seems like passing forever to the birds.

'Soiridh! Hirta!' will be hard to say when it comes. But come, apparently, it must. Then all that will be left will be the forefathers who sleep in the little God's acre, around which the fulmars well and scream and the sea is ever speaking.

Other Articles

Daily Express, 13 June 1930

ST KILDA: THE FIRST PUBLISHED PRONOUNCEMENT BY A NATIVE UPON THE EVACUATION OF THE ISLAND

The little island of St Kilda is to be abandoned – left to the birds. The announcement is not likely to disturb the mainlander seriously – at least, those of them who still cling to the belief that the axe of economy is best gripped by the head. Only those who know the island intimately will experience a feeling of regret for the step about to be taken by the last remnant of its race. To me the announcement is not only disturbing, but distressing.

It means the passing of home. It means the snapping of a chain that stretches back through the centuries. I shall be sad, as others, too, will be sad, when the last of the MacDonalds and MacQueens, the Gillieses, Fergusons and MacKinnons wave their farewell to the rock that gave shelter and succour to their forefathers for centuries. My sadness will be that of one who sees the idol of home irrevocably smashed; who will never again be permitted to sing as the vessel swings its way through the Sound of Harris –

> He, ho, soon shall I see them, O!
> Ho, ro, see them, O! See them, O!
> He ho, soon shall I see them,
> The mist-covered mountains of home!

Today the second official vessel of the tourist season is on its way. Among its passengers are two islesmen who regard the prospect of a depopulated St Kilda in much the same manner as I do. They are Mr. Alexander G. Ferguson and Mr. John Gillies. The former has for at least thirty years of a busy life been unflagging in his zeal to do everything possible for the men and women of his native isle. His home has been the St Kildians' employment exchange. Here he has kept them till work was found. No man knows the island better, or what it is capable of accomplishing. He carries a sad heart home.

The other carries too a heart that is aching. They have been told, as I too have been told, that the mainland will at least offer a chance of culture and refinement to the last of the island's race. Those who make such idle statements have yet to learn that such has ever been God's gift to the children of quiet places. The culture they are likely to find is that of the Bureau for the young folk and the parish for their elders. It is said that they might be conveniently settled upon crofts in one or other of the Outer Hebridean islands. But a crofter's existence is much the same everywhere.

Hirta is in many respects preferable to Harris. After all, it is home to my people; a home only more binding, more gripping, more endearing – even in its solitude.

I appeal to the representative of his Majesty's Government, who is now on the way, to help the last remnants of my race, not by offering them a home, which at best can never be such, but by sending a regular mail during the winter months.[101]

Science has now made yards of miles, and everybody, save the natives of St Kilda, is enjoying the benefits. There is no excuse. Even that of the island being unapproachable during the winter months is a palpable falsehood. The island is well sheltered. If the wind is from the north or west, as it variably is during the winter, then East, or Parson's Bay affords the best of shelter. Here during the height of a northern gale I have seen a dozen trawlers ride peacefully at anchor.

Should the wind veer they can make for Glen Bay or Loch-a-Ghinne, a sea loch on the other side of the island. If an

---

[101] This was a major reason for the ultimate need for evacuation, as felt by the islanders. Gillies, *The Truth About St Kilda*, 83.

arrangement could be made between the Postmaster-General and the trawler owners Association, then the troubles of lone Hirta would be at an end.

There is still another point which might materially contribute to the easing of the situation, and that is a wholesale abrogation of the existing island laws which compel the people to pay certain imposts that are—to me at least—monstrously unjust.

Is there another crofting community in the country that, after paying rent for the cottage and land, must pay to the proprietor a tax on every head of livestock? I don't think so.

Here is what my people pay to the Chiefs of Dunvegan: Thirty shillings for the croft, which includes the cottage. Seven and sixpence for every head of cattle. Ninepence for every sheep on the main island of Hirta, sixpence for those on the four miles distant island of Borrera, and, in addition, the sum of one shilling for lambs wintered on the adjacent island of Dun. I am in entire agreement with Mr. Mathieson, who, in 1927 made the first authentic survey of the island; that it might well he made a profitable island still by a little assistance from the Government to tide the people over the worst period in their history. The island's fine deposits of granite and synthite might be made into setts for the streets of the new Britain that will never be built or made by idle hands.

There is not a young man of St Kilda on the mainland today that would much prefer to shape setts from the rocks of Connachair than to shape a course to the Bureau.

There is not an old man or woman on the island but would welcome the prospect of more regular mails during the winter.

After all, the island of my sires is little different today from the larger island which nourishes and sustains us all. It has its problems that can never be solved by simply shelving them or running away from them. It flounders in the self-same quagmire of political and economic disorder as the rest of the country.

We cannot allow a single acre to go out of cultivation today without a serious effort being made to arrest it. I, therefore, hope that the Under-Secretary of State will devise ways and means of bringing to my people a modicum of the benefits that science has made possible, and spare the prospect of the "puffins," bold in the absence of man, laying their solitary egg and hatching out their young beneath the stones that mark the last resting-place of my sires.

Oban Times, 12 July 1930, Letters to the Editor

To the Editor of the *Oban Times*

ST KILDA TALES OF HIRTA, TRUE OR FALSE

Sir, As the *Oban Times* is read the world over by Gaels, I'm in hopes that you will give me—a St Kildian, and a woman—an opportunity of telling Highland folk the truth about 'Eilean mo graidh' – Hirta.

For the last year or two 'ink-coolies'[102] have been lying – lying about my little island home and its small remnant of simple, voiceless folk. Occasionally an odd honest stranger has tried to dam or divert the black, poisonous stream, but, ach, mo chreach, in vain. I lately tried myself in a Scottish newspaper, to tell Lowlanders how we in Hirta live; how few and simple are our pleasures; how intense and lasting our griefs, how pure, hardy, healthy and peaceful our way of life in the remote little isle of the sea. But

---

[102] 'Coolie', now a derogatory term, was a word for an unskilled native labourer, usually associated with the imperial possessions in India and China. The modern term for an ignorant journalist would be 'hack'.

the kindest of Lowlanders do not understand the Gael, and the 'ink-coolies' have poisoned the wells; and the Socialist Government will deport my kinsfolk, and Hirta will become truly 'the isle of the dead' – mo thruaighe! Maybe it will be a safer place for landing aeroplanes then? Maybe?

They say in the papers than my kinsfolk are now starving and terribly lonely, and longing and praying to the Socialist Government to be deported – to some Lowland paradise, I suppose? Nonsense! Food is as plentiful now as ever it was, and the people to feed, less. The birds of the rocks and the sheep of the hills are as numerous as ever. Only the fish have deserted them, driven by Sassenach trawler men to other and still remote spawning beds, where, sooner or later, the cruel steel net will find them out, only to destroy them as it has a once flourishing industry. But there is still plenty of food.

Hirta today is not more remote and lonely than it was ages ago. Today the ends of the Earth meet. Miles are now but inches, and the best that science can make of us is paupers! This Lowland paradise for thousands of Gaels is the 'Parish' and the 'Bureau'. My people don't understand. I have never heard them express a wish to be deported. I do believe, however, that such a wish has been 'put in their mouths', and that they have fallen for this 'Paradise dope' like a few millions more a little over a year ago.

When I read that Mr Tom Johnston, Under Secretary for State, is seriously concerned about the cost of the evacuation of, in all, about 34 humans beings from Hirta,[103] I feel that the Socialist Under Secretary is but making a mock of the island's day of sorrow, and is no longer Caraid nan Gaidheal, or of the oppressed. Mo chreach! mo chreach!

Alas the depopulation of the Highlands goes on, and the advocates of it will continue to find or invent false, if plausible, reasons for deporting the old race that once peopled Tir nan Beann. To make it easier, one such advocate in the person of the Socialist

---

[103] The total number would be 36.

Under Secretary has suggested that, after all, we Hirtaichs are but the descendants of a race of criminals, the island having been at one time (according to Mr Johnston) been used by the hereditary Chiefs of Dunvegan as a 'penal colony for misdemeanants'. If he doesn't know the history of Hirta, I do. God be merciful to us from the pens of those who would make history from the thin voice of tradition – a voice they don't under-stand, a speech they cannot comprehend!

I read the other day that Mr Adamson suggested that the nurse in Hirta should be honoured by the King for her inestimable service to the islesfolk. Her service was her duty, her duties her service. The real Caraid na Hirtaich has been, and is, Mr Ferguson the Glasgow tweed merchant, a Hirtach him-self. His father was bailiff of the island, as his brother is today. No one has ever approached Mr Ferguson in his devotion to the interests and welfare of the isle folk of Hirta, and all the decorations that monarchs may bestow on others will never displace Mr Ferguson in the heart's core of na Hirtaich. Looking back across the years I see, too, another in the person of our old dominie-divine, the Rev. Angus Fiddes, who, when he could not get a nurse to stay, proceeded to the mainland—to the same city as, in later years, lured me – and there took a course of maternity training, returning to his threefold task of minister, schoolmaster and nurse. He sleeps forgotten in a little churchyard of Easter Ross – Portmahomack. But happily he lives in the memory of those who, like myself, knew him as all three, and more.

I am happy to note that such able men as Compton MacKenzie, Mr Ramsay, MP and Mr Matheson, the noted Scottish geographer, give no credence to the tale that the last remnants of my race will be healthier, happier, or purer in the slums of the mainland, unemployed or casually working, that they are at the moment on 'an t-eilean a chuan' – Hirta. And thousands of Gaels will join them, and me, in condemning this or any other Government who will make Hirta an 'Isle of the Dead' and condemn it to the same fate as innumerable crofter villages now lost amongst the almost countless acres of the sportsman's paradise. Tomorrow it is in danger of becoming but an island of dreams to the exiles, a memory of joys that are past, sweet yet mournful to the soul; and all this because Governments have for the last 40 years been unheeding to our plea of better facilities during the winter – facilities that are not only the need of Hirta but of all the Hebrides, Soiridh, Hirta!

> From the lone shieling and the misty island
> Mountains divide us and a waste of sea;
> Yet our hearts are true, our hearts are Highland.
> And we in dreams behold the Hebrides.[104]

—Mrs Christina MacDonald MacQueen, Stonehouse, Lanarkshire.

Postscript 1   Letter to the Editor, 26 July 1930[105]

The Evacuation of St Kilda
[to the Editor of the Oban Times], Malaglate, Lochmaddy, 16th July 1930

Sir, – Much has been written in your popular and widely read paper on the above subject recently. There is one vital sentiment that neither time nor distance can take from the Gael, and that is his happy memories of and fidelity to his birthplace and his attachment to the land of his forefathers. No doubt the natives of St Kilda, who are attached to their native place, will have heavy hearts when the time comes to leave their island home, isolated though it be. The letter which appeared in the *Oban Times* of 12th July contained a most interesting and touching letter from the pen of Mrs Christina MacDonald MacQueen of Stonehouse, Lanarkshire, herself a native of St Kilda and fully conversant with

---

[104] Quotation from the Canadian Boat-Song
[105] These three postscripts have been included because they relate to Christina's *Oban Times* articles.

all conditions there. It is the earnest hope of all those who are in direct sympathy with the St Kildans that, when removed, they will not be separated from each other. In St Kilda they have lived in absolute harmony and peace from generation to generation, practically as one family, always sharing the same supply of meal and grocery stores and foods of all kinds, whenever and from whatsoever source derived.

It has been stated that the St Kildans were descended from a race of criminals who were sent there in bygone time, when, it is alleged, the island was used as a penal colony for misdemeanants. If this allegation be true, it is equally true that crime has been unknown there, as may be gathered from legal records. Above all, the St Kildans, according to their meagre means, contributed more to the Church Funds since 1843 than many better-off communities, as may easily be gathered from the Church records.

Since the "Apostle of the North", Dr John MacDonald of Ferrintosh,[106] who felt so much concerned about the spiritual welfare of the islanders, visited the island for the first time in 1822, they had the pure cream of the Gospel, and faithfully adhered to it. This great divine took such a warm interest in the St Kildans that he visited them on three subsequent occasions during the course of his ministry. He composed a memorable poem on the island and its people.

> Air leamsa toirt smuain mun an Eilean.
> Tha fad o'gach fearann mun cuairt.
> Ghrad dhuisg suas mo churam 's mo mhulad.
> A cuimhneachadh cunnart na t'sluaigh.
> 'S iad mar chaoraich gun bhuachaill
> A nochdas dhaoibh cluaine na iuil.
> Gun fhios ciod na taobh gus na gluais iad.
> Na'm buail iad air creagaibh na smur.

---

[106] John Macdonald (1779–1849).

And he concluded his very beautiful poem with the following "Soiridh":–

> 'S a nis mar faic mi sibh tuilleadh.
> Mo shoiridh dhuibh uile is mo ghràdh.
> Is gu math slan leibh mu dheirreadh.
> Gu àm cur na cruinne na smàl.

Others ministered to the St Kildans, among whom were the late Rev. Angus Fiddes, who was buried in Portmahomack, Easter Ross. If the St Kildans are removed from their native island home, it is earnestly to be hoped that those taking the matter in hand will see that they are made more comfortable than ever before. I am, etc.,

D.J. MacCuish

Postscript 2   Letter to the Editor, 2 August 1930:

The Removal of the People
[Station Hotel, Mallaig, 28th July 1930]

Sir. May I express my thanks to the letter you printed of Mrs Christina MacDonald MacQueen about St Kilda. Mr Tom Johnston landed on the island with a mind obscured by seasickness, and he was in no condition to appreciate the real state of affairs. A more pusillanimous admission by the member of any Government that his party was incompetent to deal with the problems of modern Scotland that Mr Johnston's statement in the House of Commons on the subject of St Kilda I never read.

Mrs MacQueen rightly says that Nurse Barclay did no more than her duty, and I would add the same of the missionary, Mr Munro. Sentimental eloquence over nurses cannot disguise the feeble handling of the St Kilda business, which is a clear sign that the town-obsessed Labour Party intends to shirk all land problems. However, my criticism of it is not inspired by the least respect for or belief in either of its two rivals. – I am etc., Compton Mackenzie.

Postscript 3   Letters to the Editor, 30 August 1930
82 Belville St, Greenock, 15 August 1930

An Isleswoman's Book on St Kilda from Donald MacLean, 82 Belville Street, Greenock – 'In this week's issue of the Oban Times appears an announcement [see introduction, p. 14] which gives me, and, I am sure, will give many other Gaels near and far, very great pleasure. I refer to a statement that the gifted St Kildan, Mrs Christina MacDonald MacQueen, is writing a book on Hirta. This is 'glad tidings' indeed, and as Mrs MacQueen has shown herself to be possessed of rare gifts we may look for a valuable and enlightening book. So far we have heard outsiders', and, in my opinion, mostly misleading notions, about the tiny isle and the ways of its folk. There are two sides to every question, and to judge wisely one should ponder both.

'I should like if Mr Calum MacPharlain, the accomplished bard, would write us a Gaelic song, and compose or adapt an air on the theme of the Last Farewell to Hirta. It would please and hearten Mrs MacQueen to have her prose sgeul of Hirta graced by the bard's 'sounds and sweet airs that give delight and hurt not'. I am etc Donald MacLean.

Interlude   Letter from Seamus Chief of Clann Fheargguis of Stra-Chur and Clann Ailpein, 19 July 1930

The Explorers Club, New York[107]

Mrs Christina MacDonald MacQueen, Stonehouse, Lanarkshire, Scotland

A charaid

Your letter in the Oban Times awakens in every Highland heart an answering echo the world over. However the only way to prevent this 'clearance' is for someone, preferably yourself, to go to Hirta with a group of the inhabitants trust and understand and explain to them just what is to become of them as expressed in the same issue of the Oban Times, 12 July, 1930 in the article 'Reported Arrangements for Removal' which is a general dispersal of the 35 – three to Tormish, to make 150 days a year (two days a week) and a small croft, the older ones to the workhouse and the women to kitchen slavery in the Lowlands! Do they realise all this? Or are they blindly being led they know not where? Let Mr Ferguson, the tweed merchant of Glasgow, mentioned in your letter, whom they know and his brother the bailiff who knows the conditions and a Gaelic-speaking newspaper man from Glasgow accompany you—it would make a great newspaper report—and after you had explained thoroughly the conditions coincident upon removal, take a vote and I am sure you will have an overwhelming refusal to go.

Draw up a paper setting forth these facts, signed by the voters and present a copy to each of the following, the Prime Minister, the M.P. for the county, the Lord Lieutenant of the County, the Secretary for Scotland. If these people of Hirta understand, they will refuse to go, even troops cannot compel them and force will be most unpopular to the public mind.

---

[107] Seamus was born in 1879, Warsaw, Poland, and died in 1961.

Like many other 'clearances', the victims of this one will mourn too late their lost freedom, their simple lives, the fulfilled wants without the worry of the city and slum dweller. What do they know of the filth, the poverty, the horror, the crime of the city and the slum? What of the unemployment everywhere? Once gone from their clean, decent island never again will they be able to return much as they desire to do so. It is the same with all of Scotland's exiles. They are lost forever. They cannot breast the tide of the present civilisation and they will sink to its dregs. Having no attachment to the new soil upon which thy will be placed, they will be unable to keep up, will drift away eventually to the slums and the streets. History repeats itself.

Please follow this course at once, you have no time to lose. If you carry this through, as you can and must, it will be the greatest achievement of your life and you will be blessed by countless generations to come. In five years navigation it'll be completely changed (isolation will cease) Is mise do charaid dileas

Clann Fhearghuis of Stra-Chur
(the chief of Clann Fhearghuis of Stra-Chur, C.M. etc).

Letter from Seamus Chief of Clann Fheargguis of Stra-Chur and Clann Ailpein, 25 July 1930

The Explorers Club, New York

Mrs Christina MacDonald MacQueen, Stonehouse, Lanarkshire, Scotland

A charaid

If there be any question of funds in proceeding to St Kilda, please let me know by cable at once. The nearest telegraph office will take your message. Address for cable: Clannfhearghuis, Explorers Club, New York. Need £? Christina MacQueen.

Looking forward to hearing directly you get this.

Clann Fhearghuis of Stra-Chur.

Hamilton Advertiser, 9 August 1930. Robert Chalmers

This is an article by Christina's husband Robert Chalmers who visited the island prior to the evacuation. The other articles in the series, which relate the journey to St Kilda, along with a selection of photographs he took, are placed in the appendices.

THROUGH THE HEBRIDES TO LONE ST KILDA PART III

With a week's supply of cigarettes, an old suit, a pocketful of photographic spools, and – 'no provisions,' I stepped ashore on the rocks of east, or Parsons bay, St Kilda, on the morning of July 15, to commence a week's investigations of the conditions obtaining on the Island on the eve of its evacuation. Having an intimate knowledge of St Kilda and its people, I paid no heed whatever to the all too frequent statements of ignorant Ink Coolies that starvation lurks in its every dwelling, and that a traveller must take with him a boat-load of provisions. Although my bag was heavy when I left, it was light when I landed. Highland hospitality has a habit of taking that turn. The natives killed for me, on the morning of my arrival, a fine, fat Wether,[108] and had a large portion of it cooked for my first meal. The friend who accompanied me[109] said, in an undertone when he saw the groaning trenchard: "Is this the place where folks are ever starving!" But I paid no heed to his question, for, like him, I had been long accustomed to the Mainlanders' morsel of mutton, and the sight of a whole roast leg fairly left me speechless.

---

[108] Castrated male sheep.
[109] Possibly David Chalmers, his father, who was with him, although it may have been another member of the party.

THE WONDERFUL WALLS OF HIRTA

With the inner man well satisfied I sallied forth to conduct my friend around the Island. St Kilda is entirely different to what a Mainlander, well fed on press verbage, might expect. It is not a barren rock, thin of soil, and scant of verdure, but a delightful little green grassy Island, some three miles long, by two miles broad, with three very high, and dominating mountains, and carrying a thousand head of sheep. The mountains are terribly steep, green from their base to their summits, and completely encircle the village. The latter consists of sixteen little grey dwellings of two apartments each, with a more substantially built house in which the Nurse resides, and a little church, manse, and school. The village is crescent shaped, with the cottages set at equal distances apart, and the whole enclosed by a dry-stone dyke, or wall, measuring fully a mile from end to end. This wall, together with that which encloses the cemetery, is perhaps the finest example in the British Isles of wall building without mortar. The same may be said, too of the stone sheep-folds between Oiseval and Connachair. Whatever the ultimate fate of St Kilda, these walls will long continue to testify to the constructive ability of its old Island race. They represent the work of centuries. They are built with stones, some of which, by their size, might well seem to have been placed in position by the hands of giants. In the company of a well-known Trades Union Official of the building industry who was a passenger with the SS *Hebrides*, I measured one of these stones in the sheepfolds of Oiseval (east fell) and found it to be six feet, by three, by two. Like me, he was amazed – not only at the size and weight of the stones, but at the excellent workmanship, and observed that, in the years to come, St Kilda's Dykes will probably be as great an attraction to tourists, as the Island is today.

OTHER ARTICLES

THE 'TENERIFE' OF THE HEBRIDES

The first thing to strike a visitor to the Island is the natural, and well sheltered bay. It sweeps around the base of the mountains in a graceful curve, as if the sea had gradually eaten its way into the very heart of the hills, only to find its further progress barred by the sharply ascending foreshore – a foreshore littered with an amazing wealth of rounded boulders, and below which, at low tide, the whitest of sand may be seen. No wonder MacAulay, the Island historian, refers to it as the 'Tenerife' of the Hebrides. It is truly a beautiful bay. Here, during a slight gale on Friday, 18th ulto. [this month], a couple of Fleetwood trawlers came into shelter. Outside the nor-easter [wind] was whipping the waves, and driving columns of salt spume towards the Island, but the trawlers rode peacefully at anchor, only going off to sea again when the wind had abated, and the waves were less boisterous. All the statements about St Kilda being terribly exposed, and wellnigh unapproachable, seem terribly overdrawn, when one sees the harvesters of the deep make a bee line for its well-sheltered bay.

THE ISLAND'S BIRDS AND RELIGIOUS WELLS

Quite apart from its antiquities – its many religious wells, and strange underground dwellings, all of which bespeak an ancient civilisation, St Kilda would be famous for nothing other than its wonderful bird life. It is the home of many species of sea birds not commonly found around our coasts. The 'fulmer', greyer in colour than the common gull, and with a bill fashioned somewhat like a parrot, literally cover its rocky ledges in millions.

Commenting on their profligacy, a well-known naturalist once observed: 'so numerous are the birds on St Kilda that it might well seem possible for them to fly off with the Island'. I had an interesting day's sport amongst the puffins (sea parrots), with a young Isles-man, and found them so numerous amongst the rocks of Gleann Mor (big glen) that I killed enough for my own dinner and that of my friends with a single shot using an ordinary single barrel fowling piece, and a number 5 Ely cartridge. At the bottom of Gleann Mor is the celebrated 'Tobar nam Buaidh' (well of virtue), the water of which was regarded by the natives of a past age as having peculiar healing powers, and to which they bent their steps in periods of affliction.[110] Associated with the well were certain rites that had to be observed else the virtue of healing would pass from the water. In the case of sickness, the party despatched to the well had to speak to no one either going or coming. Failure to observe this meant the water losing its charm. To go to that sacred well means a climb of a thousand feet over the shoulder of the 'Mullach Mor' (big hill), and a long tramp of fully a mile down a desolate glen in which there is not a shrub or tree to relieve the gloomy prospect. A long and dreary road indeed – even with company, but what a weary, dismal road it must have seemed to those early faith healers of Hirta.

ON THE GOVERNMENT'S EVACUATION TERMS

I was present on the Island when the Government's documents relating to the disposal of the Islanders' flocks came to hand. They co-opted me a member of their centuries-old Forum, and asked me to read over the terms. I did so, after which they were translated into Gaelic for the benefit of the older members. As soon as I got the gist of the documents my mind flew to the lines of Charles MacKay, the Victorian Poet, in his lament for the Highland emigrant:[111]

'Come away, far away! from the hills of bonnie Scotland;
Here no longer may we linger on the mountain or the
  glen.

---

[110] See picture in annex taken by Robert of David Chalmers and Neill Gillies (presumably the 'young Isles-man') at the well.
[111] Charles Mackay (1814–89). The song this is taken from is called 'The Highland Emigrants'.

Come away why delay? far away from bonnie, Scotland;
Land of grouse and not of hero, land of she, and not of
men!'

They were to pay for their own banishment – not only in sheep, but in tears. It was a case of sheep first, men and women afterwards. 'We will send a vessel; we will send too shepherds armed with nets and dogs; we will sell all your sheep in the market of Oban, and after we have done this, and you have paid it all, we will return for you!' As St Kildians capital has ever been his flock, and so a charitable Labour Government well knowing this, decided to make certain their migration to the Mainland, where once despoiled of their sheep, there would be little hope of ever disturbing this smug complacency; ever again torturing them with their appeals—so long made, so long unanswered—to extend the same consideration to them as Governments have ever willingly extended to the South Sea Islanders, and the savages of more distant spheres. To me, at least, those Government documents were a bitter, and tragic comment on the wisdom of our politicians when, in the face of science, and at a time when practically the ends of the earth meet, they should be parties to writing their names to another chapter in the already dark and gloomy history of 'Highland Depopulation'.

FURTHER REFLECTIONS

Granted, the young folk want to leave. But there is enough young folk workless on the mainland today without adding to their numbers. A wise Government, with the knowledge that the land problems of the country need to be squarely and fearlessly faced, would have gone out of its way to have encouraged the young men to remain and further develop the resources of an island that is perhaps the most fertile of its size from Barra Head to the Butt of Lewis.

I can well anticipate the Government's answer to any criticism of their handling of the St Kilda problem. But there is enough ammunition to beat back their counter attack in the many ludicrous examples of unjustifiable expenditure of public money. Last week a huge gas-bag, which cost a million to construct, endangered more life, and wasted more money in a single voyage to Canada, than would have assured communication with the loneliest island outpost for many years to come. To the old folk of Hirta the question of their enforced exile is a tragedy. Some of them cannot believe it. I was asked to put in two panes of glass in the skylight of a dwelling, and when I said "sure now and you'll not be needing glass in your window since you are leaving!" But he only looked at his wife,[112] and she looked at me, and I knew by that wistful expression that she'll never see any other cottage in her life but the little grey dwelling under the shoulder of mount Connacher. God be merciful to those who, in waking or in sleeping, will ever hear the sea music on Hirta's rocky shore!

---

[112] Possibly Neil Ferguson, 54 and wife Ann, 53 of number 5. The other older couple were Norman MacKinnon, 50 and wife Ann, 42, although Norman was apparently one of the first to say he wanted to evacuate when the proposition was made by Nurse Barclay. Gifford, *The Last Families of St Kilda*.

Interlude   Letters to the Secretary of State, 7 August and 15 August 1930

(Scottish Office stamped twice on 11 Aug. 1930)[113]

4 Caledonia Avenue
Stonehouse Lanarks
7/8/30

To the Right Honourable William Adamson, M.P.

Secretary for Scotland.

>Dear Sir

Might I be permitted to accompany the Government Vessel that, according to the press, is to proceed to my home, St Kilda, on the 28th inst?

I would like to see my brother and sister, and be present when the last remnants of my race bid the old home goodbye. Please let me know at your earliest convenience.

>I am sir, your obediant and humble servant
>Christina M. MacQueen

12 August, 1930

Madam,[114]

---

[113] National Records of Scotland, AF57/32.
[114] Crossed out in pencil and replaced with 'Sir'. A similar rejection letter was also sent to Donald MacQueen on 15 August 1930 (5541/108.A.). Both Donald and Christina's letters were received by the office on the 13th. The pencil marks on this letter show that it was used as a copy for the reply to Donald MacQueen (dated 15 August). Other letters were also sent by those desiring to witness the evacuation, mostly from press outlets and were similarly refused.

ST KILDA, MY ISLAND HOME

With reference to your letter of the 7th instant,[115] I am directed by the Secretary of State to say that he regrets it will not be possible to provide accommodation to enable you to be present at the evacuation of the island of St Kilda.[116]

>I am Madam,
>Your obedient Servant,
>>John Lamb.

Mrs Christina M. MacQueen,[117]
4, Caledonian Avenue,
Stonehouse,
Lanarkshire

(Scottish Office stamped 18 Aug. 1930 and 19 Aug. 1930)

>4 Caledonian Avenue
>Stonehouse 15/8/30

To the under Secretary for Scotland

>Dear Sir

I am in receipt of your favour to the 12th inst refusing me the opportunity sought of getting home to St Kilda to see the last of my people in "fair Eilean mo ghraidh".

May I not again try to move you? Perhaps you will have heard that my husband was cited as a Juror just prior to the fair holidays, and as the result of which the Law robbed me of the holiday which I had planned with him in Hirta. He went home alone. A full weeks wages were lost, together with his daily expenses travelling to and from Stonehouse to the High Courts of Justicary, Glasgow.

---

[115] Note in pencil in the margin noting 'received on the 13th inst'.
[116] 'Accommodation' here presumably refers to 'means' rather than literal accommodation.
[117] Crossed out with Donald MacQueen's address entered in pencil.

You ought to know what this means to a workers wife.

In addition, I am anxious to tell my people something about Mainland life that has not been told them, and further, to appeal to them to make Governments, of whatever colour, do their duty and save the home that was my mine and my fathers, rather than destroy it.

The whole business from start to finish has been the work of despairing Sassenachs.

Please give me the opportunity sought
Yours faithfully
Christina M. MacQueen

21st August, 1930

Madam,

With reference to your letter of the 13th instant,[118] I am direct by the Secretary of State to say that he regrets it is not possible to accede to your request to be provided with accommodation to enable you to visit the island of St. Kilda.

I am, Madam,
Your obedient Servant,
W. Hogg

Mrs. Christina M. MacQueen,
4 Caledonian Avenue,
Stonehouse,
Lanarkshire.

---

[118] The date here is perhaps a mistake and likely indicates that this letter was a copy of the one to Donald MacQueen on 15 August which starts 'With reference to your letter received on the 13th instant...'.

Oban Times, 23 August 1930.
Letters to the Editor

IT MUST NOT BE "SOIRDH HIRTA!"

How I regard the Government's attempt to break up my home: What its passing would mean

> From the lone sheiling on a misty Island,
> Mountains divide us, and a waste of seas;
> Yet still our hearts are true, our hearts are Highland.
> And we in dreams behold the Hebrides.

On the twenty-eight of this month His Majesty's Labour Government has decided to stage the last act in the drama of Hirta. On that date, with the aid of a Naval sloop and fishery cruiser, it will destroy the last exclusive outpost of the Gaelic tongue, and carry into exile the thirty-six survivors of years of Governmental neglect.

The minimum of publicity will be given the tragic event so that only those in authority will witness the grief of my people, and that the last act will not be (according to the reported statement of the Under-Secretary for Scotland) "in the nature of a Circus." People don't go readily to a Circus to witness a tragedy; they go to see the clown, to laugh, and to forget. But, *tha diofar eadar ciall is cuthach* (there is a difference between sense and madness!).

SEVENTEEN SHILLINGS PER WEEK!

As a native of Hirta, a woman, a mother with twenty-five years' experience of mainland life, I have a knowledge of the needs and aspirations of my people. They are bringing the young folks of home to introduce them to the grave uncertainties of a worker's life on the promise of a guaranteed hundred and fifty days' work per annum (three days per week), and while they do so other young natives of Hirta, amongst whom is my own brother, are trying to exist on the seventeen shillings a week – the Politician's price to save them tackling seriously the Land and other problems that confront them. Another young native who discovered it was economically impossible to pay his landlady twenty-five shillings a week from seventeen, went home on the tenth ult. in the company of my husband to his mother, leaving behind him the seventeen shillings as a Hirtach's contribution to the fund for the sustenance of our two million unemployed. *Och, mo chreach! Mo chreach!* It is sad am I, to think that never again he'll have the comfort of his mother in the cottage under Connachair.

HEARTACHE AND HEARTBREAK

The press must stay back. It must be kept dark and secret – this final breaking off of my people from centuries of associations, from the birth-place of their sires, from the cemetery of their hopes. Only the spirits that Connachair has, through the centuries, gathered to its bosom, will be allowed to gaze on the procession of broken men and women – the old folk who have no desire to leave, who never expressed any desire to leave, but who are being taken to exile, and a worse form of isolation than ever they experienced in Hirta, because of the failure of politicians to sense the needs of the moment, and make provision for the developing of the Highlands and Islands, not as mere show places, but as places fitted to nourish and sustain a happy and contented peasantry.

SOME TRENCHANT TRUTHS

I will be told that my young brothers signified their willingness to leave, appealed to the Secretary of State to be taken off the Island. But they did so under pressure – the pressure of those whose promises, I'm afraid, will turn out as shallow as their knowledge of Highland needs. These young men, largely nurtured and developed in the war period, were swept into the same quagmire of economic falsity as the whole world is presently floundering in. It was easy then for Governments to send vessels to the Island, to keep in touch with their subjects, to give them a mail almost every other week. Apparently it was a difficult matter to do so when a thousand vessels were withdrawn from service and about to be scrapped!

I will be told too, that it takes money to send a vessel to Hirta; but I will answer that it takes money to send the "Hesperus" round the lighthouses. But they will add, "the lighthouses perform a service to the sailors of the world"! And I will tell them "so has Hirta"! Many a vessel have we guided to the sure haven of our bay. Many a time in the dark nights of winter, when the winds whipped the waves to madness, and the north and west side of the Island was a thick curtain of salt spume, have we fought for the lives of despairing mariners. Sometimes we have won, sometimes we have lost.

LET US SAVE HIRTA!

The last trawler skipper to take me and my children to fair Eilean mo Ghraidh went down with his vessel in the vicinity of the Sound of Soay on the north-east of the Island three winters ago, after a memorable struggle by the natives to effect his rescue. And for all this – what? "A home for the old folk that can never be better than a prison." *Ach…mo thruaigh! Mo thruaigh!* But I refuse to believe that Hirta is doomed. The last Hirtach has not been laid in the corner under the hill. The Gaels from far and near will muster their strength to defeat the ends of those who have Hirta mapped for other things. I refuse to bring my wheel. It is left with my heart in the tenth little cottage of that straggling line to wait the day when the gloaming comes. Then there will gather round me the spirits of those who just lie sleeping, and whose voices still come to me in the night time when sleep has carried me home to fair Eilean mo ghraidh.

OTHER ARTICLES

THE SETTLEMENT IN MORVERN FOR ST KILDANS

It appears now, to be definitely arranged, that the St Kildans are to be settled in Morvern, on the mainland of Argyll. Five families are due to arrive there at the end of August. In the first instance they will be accommodated in five of the empty houses recently purchased by the Forestry Board with the Fionnary Estate. They will in consequence live at a considerable distance from one another, as the houses mentioned are far apart, viz: Savary, Achnaha, Archness, Larachbeg and the village of Lochaline. It is believed that this is only a temporary arrangement, and that the whole colony will be transferred to Larachbeg at the Martinmas Term, where they will form one community as before.

Readers of "Kidnapped" will remember that Alan Breck passed a somewhat troubled night in the Change House at Larachbeg in the course of his wanderings.

The houses destined for the Islanders are in one large block of building and are well equipped with modern conveniences – hot and cold water, cooking ranges etc. there are flower gardens in front and vegetable gardens behind the block, which is flanked by plantations of fir and spruce, and looks down on the valley of the Aline with its green crops and ripening corn.

Doubtless the migrants will find everything very bewildering at first, and it is feared that they will not easily adapt themselves to their new and strange surroundings – three miles from the sea!

[Advert placed below the article] There is one more opportunity to see St Kilda before the historic de-peopling. Messrs MacCallum Orme & Co are sending the "Hebrides" on a final cruise, leaving Glasgow on the 28th of this month. The round fare is £10, and application should be made early to the Oban Agent, Captain Duncan MacDougall, Albany Street, or to the Offices of the Company, 45 Union Street, Glasgow.

Daily Record, 29 August 1930

ST KILDA WOMAN'S TRAGIC PICTURE: SADDEST OF PARTINGS.

There is a poignant strain in the following memory, penned by a native of St Kilda, of her departure from the lonely Isle 25 years ago, which is attuned touchingly to the evacuation of St Kilda by the last of the inhabitants – *Editor.*

FIRST WOMAN TO LEAVE ISLAND: 25 YEARS AGO, AND NOW

If anyone had suggested to me on that July morning, 25 years ago,[119] when the natives of Hirta waved me their farewells, calling between the sobs, "*Christiana mo phuithar! Slan leat! Slan leat!*" That I would live to see the day when no one would stand on the rocks to wave the last remnant of my race's farewell, I would have immediately left the little boats that swung in the middle of the Bay and returned to my mother.

On a never to be forgotten morning I was about to set out for the mainland after a winter of fretting and pleading – fretting for the sights that tourists had told me lay beyond the distant peaks of Harris, and pleading with the old folks to let me go.

FIRST WOMAN TO GO

I was just turned 18 then, and the first of the island women to catch the mainland microbe. Never before had a woman of Hirta got the fever so strong in her blood as to burst the bonds of prejudice and custom, and venture forth alone. Never before had

---

[119] Christina states 1903 below, but seems to imply 1905 here. She says she was not long 18, which would be 1902/03, so 27 years.

a maiden of the island doubted the devout beliefs of the elders, that the cities of the mainland were but sinks of iniquity – modern Sodoms and Gomorrahs.

I had never seen a tree, a horse, a train, or even spent a copper. My great ambition then was to wear a hat, to have my feet encased in shoes with long high heels, to exchange my simple one-piece dress, made for me by my father, for a dress like that worn by the sassenach tourists.

PARENTS' TEARS

At first my father and mother treated my express desire as merely a whim, but, when it became evident to them that I was making certain preparations for the coming of the old SS *Hebridean*, they began to relax where hostility finally turning to tears and prayers.

Now that the last sad and sinister act in the drama of Hirta has been staged, when, for the first time in history, the cottages are smokeless under Connachair and a silence as deep as death envelops the long green fertile stretches of Gleann Mor, it is only natural that there should come to me, more near, more intensified than ever, the picture of that memorable July morning in 1903.[120]

The population of the island was then 81. It crowded down to the rocks below *tobar nam ministeir* (the well of the minister) to see me depart. I was sad then. But *och mo chreach, I mo chreach*! I'm sadder now.

I was only one mainland-smitten maiden, clutching the quarter rail of the old 'Heb', and gazing ashore through a mist of tears, trying to distinguish my mother amongst the group a fluttering shawls and handkerchiefs. But yesterday there were no fluttering handkerchiefs on the rocks below *tobar nam ministeir*. Only the spirits that old Connachair has gathered to its bosom through the

---

[120] There is some confusion in this article as to exactly when Cristina left. The printed article has 1903 here. The '25 years ago' subheading would be 1905.

centuries saw them pass – the last remnants, 36 of that 80 who, 25 years ago, wept and waved at my passing.

For me, then, there was the sure and certain prospect of return. But, now, *mo thruaighe!* such hopes are fled. For me, as for them, there can be no return – no more, no more, no more forever. Hirta, our home of old, is now but a barren rock of the sea, 'safe in its own whirlwinds, and cradled in its own tempests', an Isle of the dead.

TRAGIC PARTINGS

To know the story of Hirta – the inner story of Hirta, as handed down from father to son from generation to generation – is to know of a hundred sad and tragic partings. The Clearance of 1855,[121] for instance, of which my own father was an eyewitness, contains a chapter, sad beyond words. On that occasion 30 of the islands 110 inhabitants were removed, placed on board a fever laden sailing ship and dispatched to Australia. Amongst them were my father's kinsman and their families. By a stroke of good fortune they managed to survive what must have been one of the most frightful experiences, and landed in the country of their forced adoption almost six months later.

ANOTHER ST KILDA

Taking to sheep farming in the vicinity of Melbourne, they built themselves a homestead, calling it by the name of their native island St Kilda.[122] But the name of the homestead was destined

---

[121] It was actually 1852 and the total was 36 islanders. Christina using the term 'clearance' here is a bit strong: the islanders who left did so of their own initiative and against the wishes of the MacLeod of Dunvegan. Hutchinson, *St Kilda*, 145–7.

[122] Christina is also mistaken here, the Melbourne St Kilda is named after a yatch that had belonged to Sir Thomas Dyke Acland.

for something bigger, in the course of time it was swallowed up by the ever-spreading city of Melbourne, with the result that the name was bestowed on the new and now fashionable suburb of St Kilda, Melbourne.

Another sad parting was that of 1868, when, following a disastrous fulmar harvest in August of the preceding year, a crew of eight men and one woman were dispatched to Harris in quest of much needed victuals, the solitary woman was Betty Scott, the servant of the minister, and a native of Lochinver. She was chosen because she, alone amongst all the Islanders, could speak the English tongue.

ST KILDA NO MORE

The men were chosen (as the men of Hirta wherever chosen when a pressing need arose) by the Forum – the little Parliament that sassenach ink-coolies have caricatured as a vocal instrument for wasting time. In the crew that went to Harris then, there were husbands, brothers, lovers. They never returned. Many a time in the long nights of winter, when the cruises splattered from their rusty nails and the wind and waves made a weird an melancholy accompaniment to the purring of my wheel, have I drawn closer to the peat fire, listening to the sad stories of Hirta's tragic partings.

But *och! oOchan! mise'n duigh*! There was never a sadder parting than that of yesterday. May God forever guide the steps of those who, sleeping, will ever hear the spirit voices of those they have left behind in fair *Eilean mo ghraidh!*

Hutchinson, *St Kilda*, 125–6.

The Scots Magazine: A Monthly Miscellany of Scottish Life and Letters, Volume XV, April 1931– September 1931, 101–103

Spring in St Kilda: A NIGHT WITH THE OLD FOWLERS

[Editor of the Scots Magazine] The author of the following article is a native of St Kilda and was brought up on the island. She is the foster-sister of old Finlay MacQueen of St Kilda,[123] *who is now settled on the mainland; and she writes intimately of the island life from observant personal experience.*

There will be no one in Hirta this spring to welcome home the birds. No one – ach, *mo thruaigh! mo thruaigh*! For the first time, in at least a thousand years, no human eye will scan the horizon for the heralds of the great white army that, towards the middle of April, will be streaming in to the cliffs like snows out of the north—vast phalanxes of guillemots, razorbills, sheerwaters, puffins—birds which used to furnish us with feathers for our pillows, oil for our crusies, and flesh for our sustenance. No fowling party will this spring, in the darkness of an April night, stalk barefooted and in single file up the long hill track to Connachair – the highest cliff in the British Isles or over the shoulder of the Mullach Mor, follow the winding Rathad nan Each (road of the horses) to the saddle of the Cambir and the cliffs at the Sound of Soay. No, no! – for the fowlers of Hirt have gone. They have other work to do. Afforestation claims them – at least, some of them. Others are claimed by the bureau. This spring

---

[123] She was actually half sister to Finlay. Exactly why 'foster' is used here is unclear.

some of the last remnant are engaged in sawing logs, digging drains, and planting trees amongst the wastes of Morvern. Last spring, and in all the springs since first their sires taught them the art of fowling, these men of Hirt were men of the long rope and the lure. Men who, in the darkness of an April night, and until dawn, crept up beyond the distant Harris hills, would be grouped upon the cliff tops, while far below, with a rope round his middle, one of their comrades would sit, his body swathed in a white sheet – a lure for the birds that come in the night. There he would sit, a thousand feet above the sea, waiting, watching, listening. Up above men would talk in whispers.

AT WORK ON THE CLIFFS.

Just before the dawn the first bird would come, wearied, no doubt, with its long flight over the sea (for most of the birds of Hirt go off at the fall, some for the south and warmer climes; others, it is said, for the north and even beyond the great ice barriers). In from the sea it would fly: straight for the white spot that it fondly imagined marked the place of its last years' lodgment; the place where it mated and nested and reared its young. Then would the fowler of Hirt have work to do. Quick and deft he would use his hands. There would be no time to lose. Death must come swiftly and silently to those first heralds of a Hertach's harvest. No sooner would the bird touch the white lure; no sooner would its bright yellow webbed feet seek a landing place on the fowler's head or in his lap, than it would be instantly dispatched. Not a sound would the fowler make. Not a cheep from the bird. The others must not be warned of the trap that holds death in its coaxing whiteness. So the fowler sits and waits. The ledge at his side grows whiter with the still, warm bodies of the slain. As he waits, he hears but the muffled booming of the surf a thousand feet below – the strange sea music that is Hirt's – that music I will be hearing when the children are asleep and the night is peopled with spirits.

BRINGING HOME THE CATCH.

But the fowler must soon be ceasing his task. Already dawn is brushing the east and the gaunt forms of the Islands of Stac-An-Armin and Stac-Lee, three and a half miles from where he sits, are riding out of the shadows like monstrous water kelpies or strange wraiths risen from the deep. Nearer they seem to creep till the fowler would swear they look like strange rigged ships, their yards and spars the jagged pinnacles of rock, slashed and battered by the storms of a million years, and their sails the white guano-streaming cliffs. One, two, three he signals. Now it is all excitement on the cliff top. Whispering gives place to shouts of joy.

"How many will Donald be havin', do you think?" is the question frequently asked as fowler and catch are hauled to the top.

But Donald soon appears. The catch is laid at their feet and mutually shared. Pipes are lit if tobacco has lasted till then (for many a time in the years gone by have I seen them chew the clay of their old pipes for a taste of "thick black") then it's "down the hillside heavy laden, past the peat cairns to the village". But, ach, *mo chreach! mo chreach!* there was smoke from the dwellings then; long wisps of greyish blue smoke coiling up from the cottages of Hirt. Mothers would have their kettles singing on the fire, and fathers would be at the doors to welcome their fowler sons, and cry to them as they came down the village: "*An do mharbh thu dad?*" (have you killed anything?). And if the catch was good the old man would lay his hand upon the shoulder of his son, and say a blessing thrice o'er and tell him he was a man of Hirt.

SHARING THE TREAT.

No sooner would the fowler drop his catch at the cottage door and retire for a well-earned rest, than willing hands would carry the birds to the byre where they would be split and cleaned and plucked. That day the big pot would swing above the peat flame. The fire would be frequently stirred. Children would hover around like *Na Cearcan*[124] come for their picking, or run without bidding to the Cleits – the little conical peat cairns huddled behind the dwellings – for fresh fuel with which to feed the fire. Even the dogs would come, passing to and fro in an almost unending procession halting an instant with their paws in the peat ash to sniff the pot, or rolling their large red tongues, retreat with an air of mute enquiry as if saying: "When will they be ready?" – for the dogs of Hirt knew as well as its people the difference of a six months old fulmar just from the pickle barrel, and a plump fresh guillemot or sheerwater fresh from the cliffs. And so the dogs waited until they, too, got their share. Then with it gripped tight between their filed teeth (for every dog in the island had but stumps in its jaws, this being necessary to ensure that they would not mark the sheep when catching them), they would fly outside to the croft and make babel of the April day – worrying, snarling, barking, fighting – each for its share of the manna that always came with the spring.

LONGINGS.

It's April again. The birds return to build. And I, well – I, too, have built for twenty years; have struggled through periods of depression and unemployment to make myself a nest to rear my brood, and set their little feet upon the strange, uncertain path of life. Wearied at times with the struggle, I have sighed for the peace of home. Like the birds that fly in the night, I, too, am lured to a white spot under the hill under dun Connachair where the shadows lie deep, where sixteen of the best crofter cottages in the Hebrides are now silent, and deserted. There would I fain be. There had I hoped to be. There to close my days without the daily, hourly reminder of a world run mad; never again to see the spectres of pride and poverty stalk side by side, and to dwell once again in the cottage where a grey-haired sire and a dear

---

[124] Chickens.

and gentle mother lived and died, believing that they and their children's children would forever be "safe in their own whirlwinds and cradled in their own tempests".

The Scots Magazine: A Monthly Miscellany of Scottish Life and Letters, Volume VI, October 1931–March 1932, 378–383

Old Rachael: THE LAST OF ST. KILDA'S MACCRIMMONS[125]

The author of the following article is a native of St Kilda. In this affectionate memoir of "Hirta's most musical and lovable character," she recalls intimate scenes from the lonely island life in other years.

All that now remains of the MacCruimen dwellings is a heap of ruined masonry, a mound of unhewn stones and powdered mortar over which Nature has graciously woven a covering of green.

---

[125] Rachel (as spelled on island documents) MacCrimmon, born 1832, never married. She lived in a blackhouse, number 3, in 1901, refusing to move from it. Donald John Gillies recalled her home, entirely black within due to the open hearth in the centre of the floor. Lachlan MacDonald recalled being a boy in the church being firmly encouraged by Rachel to pay attention. A fine picture of Rachel outside her home is reproduced in MacGregor. Gillies, *The Truth About St Kilda*, 51–3. MacGregor, *A Last Voyage to St Kilda*, facing p.224. Also see *St Kilda Portraits*, 40–1, 119, 257.

Twenty paces beyond Tigh Mor it stood – and still stands for those who will be seeing it – with its dome-shaped, turf covered roof, its stout walls built of the boulders that litter Hirta's beach, and its ever-open door. This little dwelling, like its last dear old occupant, was a character – the only remaining link in the chain of strange 'black houses' that used to stretch round under Connachair. Martin, on his memorable visit of 1697, found it the first house of the village. I shall ever regard it as the last.

The dwelling nearest the sea, it was the first signpost to Hirta's past, the last barrier on the road to the south, and with Rachael alive, the final warning of the dangers that lay without. It was past its door the road wound to the beach, the bay, the boat – the boat that would be carrying us out through the Sound and on to the cities where, ever since the restless curse of the south fell upon the Isles, Gaels have been lured by the preposterous fable of the gaudy, glorious, care-free life of the mainlander. Rachael's house stood between us and the way to the cities of unrest. And, och! but it was the sore passing when she would be there at the door!

"And it's leaving us you are?" she would say, in the only tongue she knew, while her stick rose and fell on the cobbles of the path, and the tears made furrows through the peat smoor that clung to her berry-brown face. And then she would put her hands on your shoulders, and with eyes that glowed like peats aflame look into your very soul and say, in her mixture of Gaelic wrath and pity: "It will be Sodom and Gomorrah that you're bound for!" But, just to be pleasing her, you would make answer and say: "*Bi' mi air ais gu h' aith-ghwarr*" ("I'll soon be back"). Rachael would only shake her head and mutter a prayer in your ear. To her the south was anathema. It never gave back what it took. A "forger of chains" she would be saying of it, as she hugged and kissed you, knowing in her heart that the good-bye would be *slan-leit* (farewell) for ever.

Rachael's life was a mixture of joy and sorrow. Early in life she saddled a load that made her joys but only transient; and yet, throughout the long years, till death claimed her, she smiled bravely through her tears. Her love of home was steadfast. Not for all the wealth that men will be shedding the blood for, or women selling their souls, would she have passed through the sound on the south road. Had she not seen them go that way and never return? Was it not for the lure of the south and the sorrow of it that "*Phir-a-bhata*" became to her a life dirge? Was it not the way *he* and they went when in 1868, when the red was in her cheek, and the first love burned in her bosom? *Och, ochan! mise'n diugh*! and it was that same!

But he never won back. All that was left to Rachael as a comfort through the years – through the sixty long years that she waited – was the strain of "*Phir-a-bhata*," with its longing and its hope. Never had a bard's word a more fitting subject:

> My friends oft tell me that I must sever
> All thoughts of thee from my heart forever;
> Their words are idle—my passions, swelling,
> Untamed as ocean, can brook no quelling—
> O my boatman.

They say it was a Harris man who first brought the old words, with their sad and querulous melody, to Hirt; but that was in the days before the ministers barred everything but Psalms, chasing the songs that the earliest MacCruimens had lilted as if they were but the rumblings of Satan's mouth.

Whether it was or no, Rachael had early caught the strain of it, the lilt of it – and, oh, *mo chreach!* but it fitted her well. All her life she waited for her boatman. He never returned.

Long before the first tourist vessel carried the restless germ to Hirt, he sailed for the Haven of Obe that lies in the Harris sound. And seven men went with him, and a Woman, too. She was of Lochinver, they say, and had the two tongues in her mouth, speaking the strange one so well that she could long converse with the minister, Neil MacKenzie, whom she had come with to serve. But she soon learned to serve another. The name of Betty Scott was changed to Mrs MacDonald, and a pretty child she bore, which she left behind her in the care of the folks she had grown to love. And so the seven men, with the woman to make their bargains, sailed for the distant Port. But Obe was never reached, and the days and the weeks sped past. Then there came into Hirta bay three ships with the light sails spreading, and a tale that was heavy to tell. But the natives heard it, unbelieving. No, no, it, could not be! Even the remnants of clothing saturated with life's blood that had been found in a cave at Malesta, on the west side of the Lewes, would not be convincing them that the boat men of Hirt were gone. Some would be saying that they were captives on the boats that brought the tidings, and that the blood-soaked clothing was but a ruse. And others would be telling, long after round the fires, of how they heard what seemed to be like sobbing from the bowels of those light-rigged ships.

But sixty-odd years have worn the edge off the old tale, and now there be but two alive who saw the fine *Dargavel* go (for it was a new boat) and the three strange ships return. Och! but it was the black day for Hirta then! But, black as it was, there was ever a crusie of hope burning in some of the dwellings. I think I must have heard that strange, sad story a thousand times when the wheels were busy in the homes of Hirt, and when old Rachael, despite her three-score years and the weight of the sorrow that bowed her, would be hobbling in to the big carding to cheer us with her lilts.

Rachael had many songs. Some would be having the black night in them, when there's no stars, and the wind piping weirdly in Glean Mor. Some, too, would have the light of May mornings, with the lambs new-born on the hill, and the west wind kissing the waters. Most of her songs, they say, were of her own making. And I'll be believing it, too for had she not come of Dunvegan's line of pipers[126] whose notes will travel to the end of time?

---

[126] The MacCrimmons served for several generations as hereditary pipers to the MacLeods of Dunvegan.

Visitors to the deserted island in the years before the out-break of the Great War (Rachael died in 1913)[127] will remember the strange old character seated upon the lichen-covered boulder at the lower end of the village, her wrinkled, peat-tanned face almost completely hidden in the folds of a multi-coloured headshawl, while her lean, hawk-like hands, which protruded from a massive Highland plaid, gripped firmly the stick which was invariably beating out a rhythm on the cobbles at her feet. She would be counted by those visitors, no doubt, a most extraordinary old woman. Like a witch she must have seemed to some. She had no English. All she could ever master of the south was a couplet which the youth of the village taught her but a few years before she died. To those who stood to gaze at her berry-brown face she would say:

> No father, no mother,
> No sister, no brother.

She was indeed the last of her line. For a number of years before her death she existed almost exclusively upon cheese, and great chunks of it could she dispose of at a sitting. At the waulking of the tweed no one was more welcome than Rachael, for she would take up a position at the end of the board, and, with voice and stick, send the urge to our elbows. She would hurry us on with a rhythm that was impelling. It never was so much the words as the music that moved us – and yet we were a most unmusical people, and what has been said about the missionaries in this connection is only too true. Most, if not all of them, had less of the good gift than ourselves.

Noteless they moved in the life of the island. I can remember old Angus Fiddes (bless his memory!) saying to the boys, as they struggled to play tunes upon mouth-organs given them by some kindly tourists, that they were instruments of the devil, and, if persisted with, would lead them to the pit. Rachael was the most

---

[127] Actually 8 January 1914.

sensible amongst us in this connection, for though she was extraordinarily devout she still had time for an old-world lay which she would be regarding as "just as sure a ladder to her Maker as the Psalms we all loved".

As near as I can translate one of her maxims, she would say: "Spinning without music is like sinning without motive". A most extraordinary old woman, kind and lovable, and with never a word of harshness, or an ear for the gossip of the village. If you took a grievance to Rachael about anything she would just be saying "Leave it to God, dear, and He'll be straightening it out!" Rachael, like all the old Hirtachs, never looked for trouble within, but always waited in dread for it from without. Away back in the days of the Boer War she hobbled up the village to acquaint us that the enemy was out at sea behind the Dun – the island with the thousand jagged points that guards Loch Hirta on the south. It was late, and we were all abed. So sure was the old woman that the island was going to be attacked that all the women and children, and many men forbye, took to the hills behind the village. I'll never forget that night, huddled in the sheepfolds between Oiseval and Connachair. At dawn the enemy was found to be a trawler – the first to visit the island.

I write this memoir of Hirta's most musical and lovable character on a bleak December night in a little Lanarkshire village, and far from the home of my sires. A belt of firs spread their arms across the highway through which, as I write, the wind moans piteously. I find me straining my ears for the sound of breakers, and thinking... thinking of another December, long years ago, when the day was near a close. I am a scholar again in the little church of Hirt—for there was no schoolhouse then—and old Angus has just liberated the class of a dozen boys and girls. The day is almost spent. Already the peak of Connachair is lost in the shadows of approaching night. The wind is from the south, and whipping the sea to madness. Across the bay the island of Dun is a raging inferno of white breakers, licking, leaping, lashing upon its steep and slippery sides. Once clear of the glebe wall that encircles the church, stinging sheets of spray from the rollers that have missed the Dun barrier meet us in the face and lend speed to our feet. I am almost at Rachael's door when I remember her pail. I turn back to Tobar na Mineister (the well of the minister) for it. The well is exactly midway between her dwelling and the school where, every day at the back-going, I'd be leaving it. Quickly I seize it, and, with the water spilling all the way, am soon at Rachael's door. The smoke of her fire meets me first; it is turned back from the hole in the roof by the south wind, and issues in a cloud from the door.

She hears my foot and cries: "Is that you, Christiana?" and I call back: "It is that, *mo ghraidh!*" Then I enter with the pail, and see her as I have so often seen her, standing beyond the fire that smoked in the middle of the floor. As I enter, a pet ewe is eating from her hand, while round the ash-rim of the peat fire numerous cats are lazing. She soon gets me the hard biscuit (a delicacy in those days), the aid of her skirt-tails rescues the old black teapot from the heart of two glowing peats.

As she pours me my cup she'll be saying: "Its up from the south the wind is, Christiana, and it's there the devil's aye raging!" After the tea she hands me the carding pins and a handful of wool, then draws her wheel over to the fire. Soon I am making little wisps of heckled wool which I lay across her knees to be ready to her hand. She sings as she works the treadle and stretches the strand. "It will be an old song of Dunvegan", she says, as her wheel purrs an accompaniment. And then I am with Rory Mor[128] stepping out to a MacCruimen's[129] pipe.

Och, och, what can I no' see and hear tonight! But Rachael's gone now. They're all gone. Night and desolation frown on Hirt. Clach na bhinnie (the milking stone) has made its three turns in the glen, the prophecy of the old MacCruimen has been fulfilled, and the children of Hirt are now widely scattered.

---

[128] Roderick MacLeod of MacLeod, c.1559–1626.
[129] 'MacCruimen' is the Gaelic form of the name MacCrimmon.

Appendices

Appendix 1   Robert Chalmers' Other *Hamilton Advertiser* Articles

THROUGH THE HEBRIDES TO LONE ST KILDA
By Robert Chalmers

PART 1   *Hamilton Advertiser*, 19 July 1930

"From the lone shieling and the misty Island
Mountains divide us, and a waste of seas
Yet still our hearts are true, our hearth are Highland
And we in dreams behold the Hebrides."[130]

It is Sunday, July thirteenth, and the hour one-thirty p.m. Some twenty minutes ago I turned my back on the castle of Dunvegan, and made my way to this quiet retreat, high on the hillside, and overlooking the waters – the grey-blue, sparkling waters of Loch Dunvegan. Across the tree tops I can discern the red and black funnel of the S.S. *Dunara Castle* which, late last night, brought me to this romantic corner of Skye, after three days delightful sojourning in and about the Hebrides. Under ordinary conditions I would have avoided this accurate and explicit introductory note as to the locus of the writer; but when one finds a flat mossy stone giving service as a writing bureau, and gets down to it, with the air heavy with the fragrance of honeysuckle, and filled with the drowsy hum of countless insects on the wing, it is with

---

[130]   See footnote X.

all feeling that no apology is necessary for painting nature as it is. Perhaps, if I had had the *Advertiser* of yesterday, I would have forgotten, at least for a time, that I was lying beside a laughing Highland burn in the misty Isle of Skye.

THE ISLE OF SKYE

But since I cannot devote the usual Sunday afternoon to the reading of "My Weekly," I have elected to convey to *Advertiser* readers some impressions of the far flung Hebrides, in the hope that these will provide – if nothing new in the way of information, at least something along the lines of entertainment; something for a quiet hour at the fireside.

I suppose it will be some indication of the loneliness of St Kilda, as well as of the distance generally covered by the average tourist vessel, when I state that I left the Clyde on Thursday, and after crossing the Minch twice I can see no prospect of reaching the lonely Isle sooner than early on Tuesday morning.

This is occasioned by calling at so many ports en-route. From Greenock the course was set for the Island of Colonsay, which we made at six a.m., after punching our way round the Mull of Kintyre, later to find the sea quite calm in the sound of Jura. Dawn had just broken when we cleared the currents of the Mull and passed gracefully through the Sound with green grassy Islay on our left, and the long fertile stretches of Jura on our right. It was a sight not to be missed; so all the passengers were astir—earlier perhaps than some of them had been for years—watching for their first sight of the celebrated "Paps of Jura" – those mighty monarchs which keep ward over the Islands of the inner Hebrides.

COLONSAY AND IONA

All too soon Islay and Jura faded astern, to give place to the more low lying Island of Colonsay with its pretty white-washed dwellings clustering round its bays, and gleaming in the early morning sunlight like jewels on a green carpet. A little while we tarried here; sufficiently long to unload a few rolls of wire netting, and some hampers of general merchandise, then on our way again for the peered Isle of Iona. We were in the middle of breakfast when the anchor cable rattled overboard, proclaiming that we had at last reached the "Island of the Druids." I left my breakfast. I sought the vessel's rail, and looked ashore to where the ruins of St Aran's Chapel, and the rebuilt Cathedral, sat side by side on the green sward; the old and the new; yet both bearing a message of times long gone. Willingly I paid the boat-man the one and sixpence to ferry me o'er the two hundred yards to the shore. For here I would gaze (as I did) on the site of the ancient Monastery, founded by Saint Columba in the year 563 and destroyed by Norse pirates two centuries and a half later – 807. Scattered around, at varying distances, and guarded by railings, are the tombs of forty-eight Scottish, four Irish, and eight Norwegian Kings. In addition are the tombs of past chiefs of Dunvegan, lying side by side, their image carved in stone; kilted, and with their broad swords crossing their breast. I recollected, as I stood there, that in September, 1773, Dr Johnson had, in the company of his friend and biographer, James Boswell, dropped tears on these unlettered stones, and begged of his friend to be left alone for a little with his own thoughts. To stand in the midst of Iona's sacred dead, and be not the prey of emotion, is impossible – at least, impossible to those who can read, in the lichen covered fissures of its stone, the message of its first builder; its first teacher, preacher, and Saint. The present Cathedral dates from the twelfth century, was built on the site of its predecessor (razed by pirates in 807), and restored by the Church of Scotland in recent years. Reluctantly I answered the vessel's warning bell, and bade adieu to Iona, the graveyard of Kings – the birthplace of Christianity, and sought a place at the stern where I watched it fade into the shadows with its memories of other days.

The course lay now to Mull where,' after an hour's sailing, we entered a beautiful bay, to tie up later at the pier of Bunessan.

One looks ashore here, and realises why the bard of Mull extolled the beauty of his native Isle above all others. The village is as peaceful as the towering heights which surround it. There is an air of tranquil, peace, and serenity. I step ashore like a native, and sing my way to the little post office, in notes that have a new and richer meaning to my ear:–

> O, Isle of Mull is of Isles the fairest
> Of ocean's gems it's the first and rarest,
> Green grassy Island of sparkling fountains,
> Of waving woods, and high towering mountains.[131]

A little while here, then on to Tiree, which we make at the down-going of the sun.

TIREE

Tiree boasts an excellent pier, and is perhaps, the lowest-lying of all the Islands in the Hebrides. In approaching it one sees the houses before the land. It is very fertile. In the twilight I walked across its green springy turf to a croft where I regaled myself with sweet luscious milk. At eleven p.m. on Friday, we set off across the Minch for Castle Bay Barra the extreme end of South Uist. This we made at two a.m. It was like sailing into some enchanted fairyland. Entering a narrow bottle-neck we soon found ourselves in a beautiful bay surrounded by towering mountains. The moon was full, and cast its beams on the water, which rippled like molten silver.

In the midst stood Kishmulls Castle, its sides washed by the tide. It is difficult to fix the date of this, the most picturesque of all the castles in the British Isles. The ancient seat of the MacNeils of Barra, it was the home and rendezvous of the notorious pirate and sea-rover, Kishmull, whom Marjory Kennedy Fraser

---

[131] Lines taken from the song 'An t-eilean Muileach' by Dugald MacPhail (1819–87).

has immortalised in the Hebridean song, "Kishmull's Galley." Tradition avers that Kishmull was not the least particular about the prisoners he captured. These he condemned to the dungeons of the castle where, at high tide, the seat swept in upon them through the slits in the castle wall. Although the hour was early I disembarked and sat upon a rock on the sea shore waiting for the dawn. My vigil was given to musing. I could imagine Kishmull's Galley sailing into the bay with its prisoners lashed to the shafts and their groans and curses intermingling with the lusty chorus of the oarsmen ...

There goes Dunvegan's Church bell, so, I'll lay aside my script and answer its call.

PART II *Hamilton Advertiser*, 2 August 1930

Last week I wrote my first instalment of this journal while lying beside a Highland burn in the misty Isle of Skye. A week later I commenced part two seated at the open window of a little cottage in the most remote island of all the Hebrides – in St Kilda; the island that is soon to be deserted; given over entirely to the birds.

If I remember aright I closed my journal last week with a description of Castle Bay, Barra, in the early hours of Saturday, 12th July. Until I close my eyes for ever, that picture will always be present with me. Out under the walls of Kishmull's Castle we sailed, as dawn crept up the sky, throwing into relief the girdle chain of frowning mountains, into the very heart of which the sea had made its way. Peak after peak stood out like sentinels as if guarding the narrow bottleneck – our only way to the open sea.

A FAMOUS HERRING PORT

As 4 a.m. rang out from the belfry on the hill, the S.S. "Dunara Castle" slowly turned her stern on the haven of the ancient Kishmull, and headed for Loch Boisdale. Loch Boisdale, like Castle Bay, is a fishing port. Its situation, too, is not dissimilar, for one sails into it through narrow channels, twisting and turning, amongst towering mountains of grey basalt; mountains that seem entirely bereft of vegetation, and which stretch interminably, only to fade with the limit of one's vision.

At 5.30 a.m. we stole into Loch Boisdale where, even at that early hour, all was bustle and activity. Highland fisher lassies; replete in oilskin garments, sang snatches of old-world Gaelic folk songs as they deftly handled the herrings which filled the gutting tanks on the shore. While they gutted, others packed. The staccato raps of the coopers' hammers came to us over the bay as they banded the barrels down and made them ready for shipment. We took a cargo of herring here, and proceeded afterwards on our way to Loch Skipport.

WHERE TROUT ABOUND

I shall always remember Loch Skipport for the excellent drink of cream got from a kindly crofter, and also for the vision of fresh water lochs, where trout were jumping for the fly at midday.

Tourists were given two and a half hours ashore here, so a company of us set off to find the village, which we were told lay some six miles distant. The road was rough, however, and the sun scorching. In addition, horse clegs were looking for the soft skin of Sassenach travellers; so, bitten and bruised, we called a halt some two miles over the moor, and sat the remainder of the time on the shore of a fresh water loch – the largest of a chain which seemed to stretch for miles.

One could not help sighing for a rod as the trout leapt and splashed in the sun. I thought of "Straven Jock" and "Hackle" and wished they had been of the company.

MACLEOD'S MAIDENS AND THE COOLINS

From Loch Skipport we sailed for Loch Maddy in North Uist, passed the island of Benbecula, and the narrow fiords which separate it from the larger islands of North and South Uist. Sometime after tea, on Saturday, 12th July, we tied up at Loch Maddy pier, and made straight for the hotel – the only hotel we had as yet found in all our wanderings. Loch Maddy is the haunt, during summer, of anglers, for here there are numerous fresh water and sea lochs, all of which abound in trout. A couple of hours here, and then on again – this time across the Minch to Skye. It was a delight to stand at the bow and watch the "misty coolins" come creeping up out of the distance. Nearer and nearer we crept to them, until we could discern MacLeod's Maidens, the two strange and fantastically shaped rocks which guard the shores of Skye and keep watch and ward over all MacLeod's' kingdom. We had half an hour ashore in Poltiel, then on to Dunvegan.

THE LAND OF THE FAMOUS PIPERS

Twilight was deepening when we entered Dunvegan Loch, the fo'castle [forecastle] crowded with tourists all on the look out for the oldest inhabited castle in the British Isles.
"There it is!" shouted a voice, and looming over the bar it came to us, a thing of inspiring grandeur. Dunvegan Castle is perched upon a rock, the base of which is lapped by the tide. It has noble lines of architecture. One can see the old jostling the new. Tradition asserts that long e'er the MacLeods held sway in Skye, the castle was first built by, the MacKaits – now known as MacCraes.

Without the uncertain voice of tradition, Dunvegan Castle has a worthy place in Highland history, and he would be deaf indeed to the whisperings of romance who could fail to catch, on a summer twilight, the note of a distant past. There were many on that fo'castle who heard, as I heard, the notes of MacLeod's piper – the famous MacCrimmon.

Soon it faded away, however, blown off by the screeching whistle of the vessel as it slowly approached Dunvegan pier. Just on the stroke of midnight the last of the cargo was landed. A good job, too, for Highlanders won't discharge a stick on the

Lord's day. I spent Sunday in Dunvegan by going to church with a young St Kilda lad, bound for his last look at the island of his sires. After that, I wrote my diary behind the castle of Dunvegan, and had to hurriedly close it on account of the warning whistle from the vessel.

IN THE ISLAND OF HARRIS: A LINK WITH PRINCE CHARLIE

On Sunday evening we passed round to a little place called Stein, where we anchored in the bay all night, singing hymns and spending altogether an enjoyable evening. Monday morning found us once more on our way across the Minch to the island of Harris. Our first port of call was Tarbert. This is a nice town with numerous shops and a, good hotel. A half hour's sail down a long loch between rugged mountains brought us to Scalpay, where a fishing fleet lay at anchor in a well-sheltered and natural harbour. Going ashore here I was shown an old shack with a tablet affixed to it, bearing the inscription that in the summer of 1746 Prince Charles Edward (Bonnie Prince Charlie) had been secreted here from his enemies.

Hiring a boat we set out on the loch for some diversion, but I'm afraid the most of the fun was with the natives in watching the antics of two female Sassenachs endeavouring to use the oars for the first time in their life. Gee! But it was fun while it lasted!

THE RUIN OF LEVERBURGH AND FIRST SIGHT OF ST KILDA

From Scalpy we next proceeded to "Obe," now called "Leverburgh," in the Sound of Harris. Here all is ruin and disorder. Great buildings designed by the late Lord Leverhulme to meet the pressing need of a herring fishing industry for the north are falling in ruins. Hundreds of thousands of pounds must have been literally thrown away here. Splendid roadways cross a tract of land that was piled with boulders only a few years ago.

But there is no one now to use these roads. The workmen have flown, and only their work remains. We spent all night here waiting the early morning tide to pass through the Sound on the last lap to St Kilda. At 4 a.m. we passed through the Sound and at six sighted the island of Boreray. Four and a half hours later—at 10.30 a.m.—I stepped ashore on the rocks of Parson's Bay, and was greeted by Mr Neil Ferguson, the island's postmaster and bailiff, and conducted to one of the little dwellings under the shoulder of Mount Connachair.

It was a fairly good crossing, although there were many yellow faces amongst the passengers. I shall tell you in my next and concluding article all about life in St Kilda today.

Appendix 2   Robert Chalmers, *Sunday Post*, 16 June 1935

HOW I BROUGHT MY BRIDE FROM ST KILDA
By Robert K. Chalmers

[see Plate 7]

The Island of St Kilda is in the news again. Smoke is rising once more from the old manse above the jetty, from taigh-mor (the big house), and from two at least of the sixteen little cottages that lie crescent-shaped under Dun Connachair. The red ensign, struck on the 29th August, 1930, is once more flaunting in the breeze below Tobar-Nam-Meinister (Well of the Minister), telling French luggermen and English trawlermen, or other adventurous mariners who must seek the shelter of Village Bay, that the Laird of Hirta is home.

To me, the announcement is of more than passing interest, for it recalls that distant July morning in 1911, when, at 2 a.m. I was rowed across Hirta Bay in the company of several bearded islanders, and conducted into the presence of a dear old woman whose daughter I was there to seek in marriage. Never, till my dying day, shall I forget the nerve-wracking experience.

Being the first mainlander to screw up enough courage to rob the little commune of one of its daughters, my appearance was hailed with considerable doubt and misgiving. Although a Scot, I was merely regarded as a Sassenach. I had, by the way, met the lady in Glasgow.

Happily, I had with me the (now) Rev. Donald Ferguson, of Scalpay, Harris, brother of the veteran tweed merchant, who is on the lone isle supervising the manufacture of a special piece of cloth for His Majesty the King, and he and the lady of my choice soon saw me through my difficulties.

ABOARD A WHALER

A week later, after the most enjoyable holiday of my life, I was en route for west Loch Tarbet, Harris, on board a Norwegian whaler, accompanied by the woman who is now my wife and the mother of my four children, with the blessings of 82 inhabitants ringing in my ears.

The whaler, which was entirely manned by Norwegians, was commanded by a Captain Christensen, a tall, red-whiskered son of the fjords, who had only an occasional English word in his vocabulary.

The vessel had four whales in tow, dead, of course, and so inflated to give them buoyancy that their humps were visible to all the winged creatures of the surrounding islands. These swooped down upon the dead whales in battalions, presumably to feed upon the sea lice which covered their hides.

APPENDICES

THE STORM

We were just approaching Stac-An-Armin, a huge pyramidical rock that rises to a height of almost 700 feet, and white and menacing with its millions of solan geese and gannets, when the wind sprang up from the south west. It was charged with rain, too, and stung the cheek like the lash of a carter's whip. In a few moments the little, evil-smelling tub was as drunk as it is possible for a vessel to get. It shuddered and staggered and rolled and plunged, swallowing seas at the one bulwark and vomiting them at the other.

My future wife and I were on the bridge when it struck us. In a twinkling the skipper was electrified into action. He got the future Mrs Chalmers into the small charthouse adjoining, and had the crew fix two hastily-provised shores across the doorway to keep her, I suppose, from being pitched out.

Next he passed a rope round my middle, making the other end fast to a stanchion, and in this position I had to remain for 24 hours, the unwilling companion of a big, red-bearded son of the fjords, whose speech I could not comprehend.

It took us altogether 26 hours to cross from Hirta to West Loch Tarbert, Harris – an experience we both hope never to have again.

One thing, however, we can never forget – namely, the kindness of the skipper and his crew. A little fellow, at the peril of his life, kept bringing hot coffee to us throughout the storm. How or where he made it under such circumstances fairly beat us to know.

Following our safe arrival in Harris, we were met at the old whaling station by Mr Harlofson, the owner, also a Norwegian, who explained in excellent English that the time taken and the inconveniences suffered on the voyage were due to the shipper's desire to bring his four whales to port. 'He might have cut them adrift' said Mr Harlofson, then added with a twinkle in his eyes, 'but whales are not so easily captured'.

Appendix 3 Notes on the Images

While Robert Chalmers was visiting St Kilda with his father in July 1930 he took a number of photographs and sent postcards to relatives; a small selection of these can be seen in plates 1 to 10. These pictures, along with others taken by other photographers and possibly some from previous visits with Christina, he quickly developed into lantern slides, from which he gave several lectures over 1930 and 1931. One, to the Larkhall Branch of the Lanarkshire Highlanders' Association, was entitled 'Through the Hebrides to Lone St Kilda in Picture Song and Story'. He told the tale of his journey in similar vein to the *Hamilton Advertiser* articles:

> in rapid succession picture after picture passed on the screen, each illustrated with fitting remarks. The old religious wells of the island, the heetling cliffs, white with millions of sea birds, the village, the church, and all the other islands and stacks of the group flickered before the eyes of the interested audience... St Kilda from a historical, geological and literary standpoint was magnificently dealt with. This, of course, was just what one expected from the husband of Christina M. MacQueen, the native woman whose articles on St Kilda appeared in the Advertiser about a year ago and before the daily press had its interest aroused'.[132]

These slides were deposited in the NRS by David Chalmers (1913–2017), who had acquired the pictures from his father. The selection of images here were printed and bear hand-written annotations. They were in the trunk described in the Preface. The slides in the NRS are more extensive, contain duplicates to ones found here, but also variations of some of them.

---

[132] *Hamilton Advertiser*, 29 November 1930.

APPENDICES

Notes on the Plates

PLATE 1: This commercial postcard was sent to Miss Agnes Chalmers, c/o Buchanan, 15393 Fairfield Avenue, Detroit, USA, and bears a St Kilda postmark. The message reads: 'St Kilda, Wed July 19, 1930. Dear Sister, This has been the best day of my father's life. For food he has had abundance mutton, fish, eggs, scones, milk. Yesterday we were in Glenn Mor shooting sea parrots. Killed 20. Great sport. Father was a great sailor coming. Everybody but he was sick. Write you later. Bob [Chalmers]'.

Agnes Chalmers was born in 1896 in Inverkeithing in Fife. Although she was in the USA in 1930, she seems to have returned to Scotland, as she died in the Fife and Kinross Asylum in 1942 (1891 and 1901 census; Fife and Kinross Asylum Register, 1922–37, 76).

PLATE 2: David Chalmers (1860–1946) and Neil Gillies (1896–1989). The editors' sincere thanks to John Gillies for the identification of the latter. Taken Tuesday 18 July 1930 (see above). This is at Tobar nam Buaidh, the Well of Virtues. Neil was the third son of John and Annie Gillies (née Ferguson), the brother of John Gillies, who married Christina's sister Mary. Neil had left St Kilda for Glasgow in about 1924 and worked in the Napier shipyard in Old Kilpatrick with Christina's brother Donald (Gillies, *The Truth about St Kilda*, 18).

PLATE 4: A commercial postcard with a St Kilda postmark of 21 July 1930, sent to Miss Donald Buchannan of 15393 Fairfield Avenue Detroit, USA (the same address that Agnes Chalmers was staying, see the Fulmar postcard above). The message reads: 'Dear Donald and Eff, Having great time in lone St Kilda. Took five days to come. Father was a good sailor – never up nor down. Love to all. Bob.'

The photographs in the postcard were taken in about 1903. Some of the individuals in the bottom left are identified in David

Quine's *St Kilda Portraits*, 58. Finlay MacQueen is the second from the left in the back row, and next to him on the right is Alexander Ferguson. The last man seated on the right is the minister, Angus Fiddes, whom Christina mentions several times.

PLATE 9: The cattle were removed from St Kilda on the *Dunara Castle* on 27 August, two days prior to the evacuation. Although the Chalmers were on Hirta until at least 31 July, it does not seem likely that they stayed until the final evacuation, so the bull may have been taken away beforehand, separately. If the Chalmers had stayed until the end they would have left that day on the *Dunara Castle*, with the rest of the islanders leaving on the 29th on HMS *Harebell*. (Steel, *The Life and Death of St Kilda*, 18; MacGregor, *A Last Voyage to St Kilda*, 292–3).

PLATE 10: Finlay MacQueen, Finlay Gillies, Donald Gillies, Norman MacKinnon (with board). With thanks to John Gillies for identifying these individuals. This is the coffin for 22-year-old Mary Gillies, who died on 21 July 1930 at 14 Main Street. The men here had collected planks to make her coffin, which they subsequently painted black (Hutchinson *St Kilda*, 286). Further photographs are found in the NRS lantern slide collection (GD000101488-00078).

Postscript

1930–1959

Writing this book on Christina has come about twenty years too late, as all those that knew her have died and her memory is lost among the other family members.

After the momentous events of 1930, Christina fades out of the public record. In April 1931 she was in communication with the Highland and Agricultural Society of Scotland asking about the St Kilda Fund, which had been used in the past to give assistance to the inhabitants of the island for the supply of flour, oatmeal and occasionally boats.

Robert appears a little more often. In 1932 he gave talks on Robert Burns to the Cooperative Educational Committee at Brechin.[133] He was heavily involved with the Stonehouse Male Voice Choir, being conductor in 1939 when he was presented with an electric reading lamp and clock by members of the choir in appreciation of his services.[134] In 1948 he is recorded as a freemason.[135]

Robert Kinneill Chalmers died on 5 July 1957, aged 68, and was buried in the grave in Stonehouse church where the 2-year-old James had been laid to rest in 1926. Christina died on 16 March 1959, aged 75 and was buried in that plot. Their eldest daughter, Janet Marion 'Jenny', who preserved a core of the documents gathered here, was buried in the same place in 1995.

---

[133] *Angus Herald*, 29 January 1932.
[134] *The Sunday Post*, 9 April 1939, p.5.
[135] *Dundee Courier and Advertiser*, 26 January 1948.

Bibliography

Andrew Fleming, *St Kilda and the Wider World* (Windgather Books, 2005; reprint 2016)

Andrew Fleming, *The Gravity of Feathers: Fame Fortune and the Story of St Kilda* (Birlinn, 2024)

Angela Gannon and George Geddes, *St Kilda: the Last and Outmost Isle* (Historic Environment Scotland, 2015; paperback edition 2016)

Elisabeth Gifford, *The Last Families on St Kilda* (St Kilda Club, 2020)

Donald John Gillies, *The Truth About St Kilda* (Birlinn, 2019)

Mary Harman, *An Isle Called Hirte: a History and Culture of St Kilda to 1930* (MacLean Press, 1997)

Norman Heathcote, *St Kilda* (Longmans, 1900)

Roger Hutchinson, St *Kilda: A People's History* (Birlinn, 2014)

Maureen Kerr, *George Muray: A Schoolteacher for St Kilda, 1886–87* (Islands Books Trust, 2013)

Kenneth Macaulay, *The History of St Kilda* (1759)

Campbell McCutcheon, *St Kilda: A Journey to the End of the World* (Tempus, 2002)

Calum MacDonald, *From Cleits to Castles: A St Kildan Looks Back* (Islands Book Trust, 2010; 2020 edn)

Alpin MacGregor, *A Last Voyage to St Kilda* (Cassell & Company, 1931),

Charles MacLean, *Island on the Edge of the World: The Story of St Kilda* (Canongate, 1972; 1992 edn.)

Martin Martin, *A Late Voyage to St Kilda* (1698)

David A. Quine, *St Kilda Portraits* (Dowland Press, 1988)

Michael Robson, *St Kilda: Church, Visitors and 'Natives'* (Island Books Trust, 2005)

George Seton, *St Kilda* (Birlinn, 2019)

Tom Steel, *The Life and Death of St Kilda: the moving story of a vanished island community* (Harper Press, 1975, 2011 edn)

Geoffrey Stell and Mary Harman, *Buildings of St Kilda* (RCAHMS, 1988)

Francis Thompson, *St Kilda and other Hebridean Outliers* (David & Charles, 1970)

Index

Acland, Thomas Dyke 96n
Adamson, William, Secretary of
    State for Scotland 12, 125–6,
    129
apples 45–6, 94
Australia 96, 134–5

bannocks 69
Barclay, Williamina 12, 112, 115,
    120, 124n
Barr, James 84
bees 96
birdlife 22, 33, 40–1, 60, 79, 89,
    93, 121
    see also fowling, puffins and
    fulmars
Boreray 17, 23, 99
Boer War 145
Boswell, James 56, 59, 74, 151
British Empire 27, 67
brochan 53

Cameron, John 28
Cameron, Mary 16
Carn Mor 44, 60
cattle 48–53, 109, 162
ceilidh 29, 34
census
    1881 1
    1891 2–3
    1901 5, 7
    1911 1, 7, 10
Chalmers, Agnes 160–1
Chalmers, David 8, 13–14, 119,
    160–1

Chalmers, David (Christina's son)
    9, 11, 160
Chalmers, Donald 9
Chalmers James Ramsay
    MacDonald 9, 163
Chalmers, Janet (Jenny) 9, 11, 163
Chalmers, Nora 9
Chalmers, Robert Kinneill
    (Christina's husband) 8–9,
    11, 13–14, 39, 42, 59, 98, 126,
    160–3
    Articles 119–24, Appendices 1
    and 2
Chalmers, Robert (Christina's
    son) 9
Chalmers, Violet 9
Chi mi na Mor-bheanna 28, 107
Chiesley, Rachel, Lady Grange
    39–40, 57–8, 86–7
clearances 6, 96, 117–18, 122–3,
    134
cleits 23, 40, 51, 86, 139
Connachair 23, 30, 33, 37–8,
    40–1, 44, 49, 60, 81–2, 85,
    136
cruises 30, 89
cuckoo 61

Dargavel (ship) 143
dogs 42, 139
Dun 6, 38, 49, 53, 61
Dunara Castle (ship) 23, 149, 162
Dunvegan 30n, 56–7, 153, 155
    see also MacLeod of Dunvegan;
    taxman

Emden (ship) 62
English (language) 5, 135
epidemics and illness 3, 7, 29–34, 90–3
Erskine of Grange, James 39–40, 57, 86–7
Erskine, John, Earl of 39, 57, 86–7

feathers 31, 43, 58
Ferguson, Ann *see* MacQueen, Ann
Ferguson, Alexander 6–7, 95, 107–8, 112, 117, 158, 161
Ferguson, Donald 8, 95, 98, 158
Ferguson, Neil, 38, 95, 98, 124n
Fhearguis, Seamus Clann 13, 117–18, 125
Fiddes, Angus 2, 5, 38n, 43–4, 46–7, 94, 112, 115, 144, 161
First World War 9, 11, 24–7, 82, 130, 144
    U-boat attack 61–5
fishing 5, 31, 45–6, 60, 111
Fleetwood 24n, 39, 121
fowling 33, 61, 82–3, 88–9, 102, 136–40
fulmars 30n, 41, 43–4, 60, 86, 103, 135, 139

Gaelic 3, 5, 14, 17, 28, 36, 42, 56, 95, 99, 135, 141, 144
Gibbons, Alfred W, or de 32
Gillies, Angus 4
Gillies, Annie 9
Gillies, Annie *see* MacQueen
Gillies, Donald John 15–16, 93n, 98
Gillies, Ewen 82–3
Gillies, Flora 16
Gillies, John 10, 12–13, 16, 72, 81, 98n, 107, 161
Gillies, Kirsty 4

Gillies, Mary (nineteenth century) 4
Gillies, Mary (Christina's sister) *see* MacQueen)
Gillies, Mary 14, 162
Gillies, Neil 15, 161
Gillies, Norman John 10, 12–13
Gillies, Rachel Annie 24n
Glasgow 7–8, 10, 12–13, 16, 24, 43, 47, 73–4, 85, 97–9, 126, 158
Gleann Mor 48–51, 53, 121–2, 143
Goas, Peter 35–6
Goldsmith, Oliver 21
Grange, Lady *see* Chiesley, Rachel

ham 44–5, 94–5
Harris 23, 31, 47, 56, 64, 70, 85, 92, 102, 108, 135
Heathcote, Norman 5, 26n, 39n, 61n, 85n
Hebridean (ship) 23, 85, 133
Hebrides (ship) 14n, 23, 90, 98, 120, 131
Hesperus (ship) 130
Hilda, Saint 36
Hogg, W. 127

Iona 22, 56, 102, 150–1
infant mortality 1–2, 9, 47

Johnson, Samuel 54–9, 73–5, 151
Johnston, Tom, Under Secretary of State for Scotland 12, 110–12, 115, 126–8
journalism 110–11

Kruschen Salts 46

Lamb, John 126
Largs, battle of 56
Lochmaddy 50, 54
lock jaw *see* infant mortality
London 24, 30, 32, 54, 59, 95

INDEX

Loudon Hill 37

MacAulay, Kenneth 35–6, 37n, 58–9, 101, 121
MacCrimmon, Mary 4
MacCrimmon, Rachel 3, 14, 29–30, 140–6
MacDonald, Ann (eighteenth century) 4
MacDonald, Ann 4, 6
MacDonald, Calum 4n, 16
MacDonald, Catherine 2
MacDonald, Christina *see* MacQueen, Christina
MacDonald, Donald 81n
MacDonald, John 2
MacDonald, John 80n, 82–3
MacDonald, Lachlan 16
MacDonald, Margaret 47
MacDonald, Marion (Christina's mother) 1–2, 4–5, 7, 9, 47
MacDonald, Margaret 2
MacDonald, William 4n
MacKay, Charles 122
MacKay, John, minister 1n, 4–5
MacKenzie, Compton 112, 115–16
MacKenzie, Neil 142
MacKie, Janet 8
MacKinlay, Ann 1n
MacKinnon, baby 2
MacKinnon, Christina 2
MacKinnon, Neil 81
MacKinnon, Norman and family 124n, 162
MacLachlan, Alice 6n, 17, 80n
MacLean, Donald 116
MacLeods of Dunvegan 3, 22, 31, 56–7, 87, 109, 112, 134n
MacLoed, John, minister 11
MacLeod, Neil 43–4
MacLeod, Norman Magnus 56
MacLoed, Rory Mor 58, 146
MacQueen, Ann 2, 98n
MacQueen, Annie 16

MacQueen, Christina (Christina's niece) 83n
MacQueen, Donald (I) 3–4
MacQueen, Donald (II) 2, 4
MacQueen, Donald (III) (Christina's father) 1–5, 17, 42, 80–1, 134
MacQueen, Donald (IV) 3, 5, 9, 14, 125n, 161
MacQueen, Finlay (eighteenth century) 4
MacQueen, Finlay 4, 10, 13, 39, 65, 136, 161–2
MacQueen, John (eighteenth century) 4
MacQueen, John 5–6, 10, 61, 80–1
MacQueen, Malcolm (and family in Australia) 96–7
MacQueen, Norman 2, 5–6, 10, 61, 80–1
MacQueen, Mary (Christina's sister) 5, 7, 10, 12, 16, 72–5, 97–9, 161
MacQueen, Mary Ann 4n
Macquin 4, 103
Martin, Martin 35–6, 54–5, 59, 101, 141
milking 48–53
Morvern 131
Mullach Mor 9, 23, 33, 122, 136
Mullach Gael 49
Munro, Dugald, minister 11, 115
Murray, George 2, 16–17, 23n, 85n

Napier Commission 5
New Year 46, 66–9
Norma (ship) 72

oil from sea birds 30–1, 89, 94
Oiseval 33, 38, 49, 53, 62–3
Old Kilpatrick 7, 10, 15, 161

Pan, Peter 23

167

peat 23, 29, 34, 40, 42–3, 45, 48–9, 51–2, 70, 81, 86, 88, 96, 135, 138–9, 141, 146
post office 38, 152
Prettyfoot 49–50, 53
puffins 41–3, 110, 121–2

quarrying 109
Quine, David 15–16

Rathad nam Each 136
Robert II 35
Robert Hadden (ship) 22
Rogers, James Edwin Thorold 32
Royal Navy 8, 63–4, 128, 130
Ruival 60

Sands, John 39n
Scott, Betty 135, 142–3
sharks 84
Shearer, Alexander 12, 72–3
sheep 13, 42, 51–2, 58, 86, 109, 119, 123, 134, 146
St Kilda
  burial ground 3, 30, 71, 103, 130
  communications 5, 8–9, 23, 31, 108–9
  fashion 26, 88, 133
  Forum ('Parliament') 13, 122, 135
  Fund 163
  houses 1, 3–4, 38, 92n, 120, 140–1
  mailboat 39
  name 35–6
  population 3, 7, 10, 21, 25–7, 29, 34, 67, 71, 74, 90, 99, 133–4
  religion 8, 88, 142, 144–5
  schooling 5
smallpox *see* epidemics
Soay 17, 23, 37, 41

Sodom and Gomorrah 24, 133, 141
spinning wheels and spinning 3, 29, 86, 92, 145–6
Stac an Armin 3, 33–4, 91–2, 138, 158
Stac Lee 138
Stonehouse 9, 37, 59, 127, 163
Stuart, James 7
sugar 44, 52, 93, 101
Sutherland, Joseph 59
sweets 24, 46, 85n, 86

taksman/taxman 31, 33–4, 39–40, 58, 91, 94, 109
taxes 24, 100–1
tea 44, 50, 67, 82, 93–4, 101, 138, 146, 154
Tigh Na Banagaisgh 49, 53
Tigh Mor 141
Tinto 37
Tir nan Beann 111
tobacco 26, 38, 44, 65, 94, 101, 138
Tobar Childa 36, 37n
Tobar Nam Buaidh 49, 53, 85, 122, 161
Tobar Nam Ministeir/Meinister 133, 146, 157
tourists 84–6
trees 24, 70, 95–6, 133, 137
tweed 7, 31, 48, 88

Victoria, Queen 61

Walker, captain 45–6, 94
waulking 15, 48, 88, 144
weaving 3, 29, 86
  see also tweed
whales 80, 84, 158–9
Whitby 36
White, Henry 74